PENGUIN BOOKS

Something More

Jean Grasso Fitzpatrick has written articles on child development and family life for such publications as *Parents*, *Working Mother*, *McCall's*, *Family Circle*, and *The New York Times Magazine*; she is also the author of three previous books. As founder of Generation to Generation, an ecumenical network for families' spiritual nurture, she gives frequent lectures and workshops. She lives with her husband and two children in Westchester County, New York.

PENGUIN BOOKS

Something More

Nurturing Your Child's

Spiritual Growth

Jean Grasso Fitzpatrick

PENGUIN BOOKS

PENGUIN BOOKS
Published by the Penguin Group
Viking Penguin, a division of Penguin Books USA Inc.,
375 Hudson Street, New York, New York 10014, U.S.A.
Penguin Books Ltd, 27 Wrights Lane,
London W8 5TZ, England
Penguin Books Australia Ltd, Ringwood,
Victoria, Australia
Penguin Books Canada Ltd, 10 Alcorn Avenue, Suite 300,
Toronto, Ontario, Canada M4V 3B2
Penguin Books (N.Z.) Ltd, 182–190 Wairau Road,
Auckland 10, New Zealand

Penguin Books Ltd, Registered Offices:
Harmondsworth, Middlesex, England

First published in the United States of America by
Viking Penguin, a division of Penguin Books USA Inc., 1991
Published in Penguin Books 1992

1   3   5   7   9   10   8   6   4   2
Copyright © Jean Grasso Fitzpatrick, 1991
All rights reserved

Chapter 9 of this book first appeared in *Parents Magazine*.

Page 239 constitutes an extension of this copyright page.

THE LIBRARY OF CONGRESS HAS CATALOGUED THE HARDCOVER AS FOLLOWS:
Fitzpatrick, Jean Grasso.
Something more : nurturing your child's spiritual growth / Jean Grasso Fitzpatrick
p. cm.
ISBN 0-670-83706-7 (hc.)
ISBN 0 14 01.6951 2 (pbk.)
1. Children—Religious life. 2. Child rearing—Religious aspects—
Christianity. I. Title.
BV4571.2.F58 1991
248.8′45—dc20 90–50516

Printed in the United States of America
Set in Perpetua
Designed by Liney Li

To all the children

Acknowledgments

*T*o all the parents and children who shared their thoughts and questions for this book, many of whom wished to remain anonymous, my deepest thanks. I am grateful to Jane Baron Rechtman for her insights and expertise; to Rick Parks, Alice Kossin, Brooke Beebe, Tina Mayas, Resa Mestel, Beth Morrison, Ann and Matthew Costello, Chris and Mitch Miller; to my friends in the 1989 spirituality group at All Saints' Church in Briarcliff Manor, New York; to the Reverends Janet Vincent-Scaringe and Steve Yagerman; to the staff and membership of Teatown Lake Reservation in Ossining, New York; and to the Ossining Public Library.

Thanks to my colleagues in the Hudson Group for advice and camaraderie, and especially to Eugene Ehrlich for many helpful suggestions. I thank Lorraine Rocissano, Ph.D., for her sympathetic and authoritative reading of the manuscript. I am grateful to my agent, Heide Lange, for her thoughtful advice and warm encouragement throughout the writing; and to Mindy

Acknowledgments...

Werner, my editor at Viking, for sharing a vision of the project and for quietly and constructively keeping me from straying from it.

Without the friendship and support of students and faculty at Maryknoll School of Theology, this book would not have been written. Thanks to Ralph Buultjens, who first suggested that I expand portions of the present manuscript—which had somehow made their way into a paper on Eastern spirituality!—for publication; to Marie Giblin and Kathleen O'Connor, whose exciting teachings on feminist theology reassured this mother that parents do theology, too; to Jim O'Halloran, director of the library; and to Ann Loretan, Mark Chmiel, and all the other students who have taught me and shared so much.

To the members of St. Paul's-on-the-Hill, Ossining, and the Reverend Philip B. Kunhardt III, thank you for your warm support. And to parishioners and clergy of St. Mary's Church, Scarborough, New York, thank you for these years of learning and exploration. Thanks to the Sunday school students who survived all of my experimenting; and to Karen and Bob Kennedy and other members of our small group. Special thanks to Ann Thurm and Dale Bennett, faithful spiritual companions; and to my friend Hillary Bercovici, who offered intellectual, spiritual, and practical help at every stage of the manuscript.

I am grateful to my cousins Tom Grasso and Bobbi Jensen, and to Joe Jensen; to my brother, Louis Grasso; and to my mother, Jean Grasso, who provided emergency child care as well as encouragement. For my children, Matthew and Laura, who are a daily inspiration, and to my husband, Des, whose steadfast love and support are a constant blessing, I offer thanks. And for the privilege of writing this book (with all its flaws) and the strength to bring it to completion, I thank the One whose children we all are.

Contents

Contents...

Something More

1. The Journey Begins

As the little prince dropped off to sleep, I took him in my arms and set out walking once more. I felt deeply moved, and stirred. It seemed to me that I was carrying a very fragile treasure. It seemed to me, even, that there was nothing more fragile on all the Earth.

—THE LITTLE PRINCE,
ANTOINE DE SAINT-EXUPÉRY

You gaze at your baby's round, soft face in the glow of the night-light. You watch your toddler clunking along the hallway in Daddy's shoes. Or you walk to the bus stop with a five-year-old whose eyes shine with nervous anticipation on the first day of kindergarten. For any parent, these are the times when a child's innocence and vulnerability are almost unbearably precious, times when we are achingly aware that he or she is, like the Little Prince, "a very fragile treasure." They are the moments that make parenting, despite its endless drudgery, so deeply rewarding.

These wondrous moments are glimpses of something more, as well. For sensible, well-organized people like us, they offer

1

windows on a new reality. It is one whose dimensions and value—unlike, say, the length of the pregnant uterus, or the timing of a child's developmental milestones—cannot be measured or plotted on a chart. These moments might be called "revelations" of sorts, revelations of a beauty and generosity at the heart of life that is deeper and more mysterious than we may have ever imagined. In struggling for ways to describe it, we may find ourselves resorting to words that do not often come to our lips. "The first time I held Ben curled against my shoulder and felt his breath on my neck," a new father told me, "heaven opened to me."

"To see my kids is to realize they are—well, godlike," said a mother of two boys, ages five and seven, "not because they're particularly unusual children, but because I could not with my own two hands have created anything as wonderful or amazing as they are." She remembered a recent pillow fight that had ended with a family snuggle under the covers. "Just tickling their feet and hearing them giggle—that's cosmic," she said. "That's divine."

Of course, not *all* our moments of revelation are quite so exhilarating. We also find ourselves reexamining our priorities when we become parents because we *have* to. Now there is a small person in our household who eats, sleeps, walks, talks, and empties both bladder and bowel according to his own timetable. Thanks to our child, we can no longer believe (if we ever really did) that everything in life can be planned, scheduled, or managed. Quite a lot seems to defy explanation.

"I was an agnostic for most of my adult life," said Marcia, a psychologist with a four-year-old son. "Spirituality seemed to be something that didn't fit into the rational world I encountered in college and graduate school. But after Danny was born, I was so worn out that my brain just was not able to focus on anything. That can be a good place to be, because you're so *empty*. I was so depleted that I gave up trying to control everything, and at some point I knew I needed to get in touch with my true source—my *spiritual* source."

Although we may not put it into so many words, in becoming parents we have embarked on a spiritual journey.

Father in heaven: When the thought of Thee wakes in our hearts let it not awaken like a frightened bird that flies about in dismay, but like a child waking from its sleep with a heavenly smile.

—*Søren Kierkegaard*

The arrival of a child is almost always a discovery of miracle. It remains a joy to remember. I can still recall how, the first time I was sure I was pregnant, I made the rounds of bookstores and libraries, scouring every pregnancy manual I could get my hands on. I got a virtuoso's training in every breathing technique known to childbirth educators. This would be the kind of "birth experience" I had prepared for, I had decided—a Lamaze performance par excellence.

Then along came the first twinges of labor. We drove to the hospital, the hours dragged by, and soon I was too worn-out to huff and pant according to plan. But lo and behold, our nine-pound baby steadily inched its way down the birth canal, and in my heart the realization suddenly dawned: "*I'm* not doing this!"

All at once I felt a peace, a groundedness, I had never known before. For the first time in my life, instead of drawing strength from the accomplishments that might set me *apart*—the Ivy League scholarship, the bylines in national magazines, the exotic cooking—I felt the power of my *connection* with other mothers and their babies all over the world. There in the labor room I felt the unmistakable presence of a force I could not name—a protective, loving force surrounding the baby and me. I had come home. And in the overwhelming moments when I first held the child close—the cord still connecting us, and his body slippery with vernix—I found myself knowing for the first time that there was "something out there."

We named the child Matthew, "gift of God."

Ever since those extraordinary moments, the deep-rooted awareness of all life as a gift has grown within me. And no wonder. Those wide eyes, soft hugs, and sloppy kisses are daily reminders of miracle. It wasn't until I became a mother that I could understand why the Italians often refer to a small child as *una creatura:* how brightly the beauty of creation shines in one so young!

Yet isn't it true that the loveliest moments we share with our children are also our most aching ones? When we are stepping off a curb together and a small hand reaches up to grasp my own, I feel the trust in those warm fingers. But it does occur to me that one Saturday night in the not-too-distant future, this same hand will be reaching out for my car keys.

And yes, we all delight in our children's budding fascination with dinosaurs and space stations, but we know not everyone grows up to be a paleontologist or an astronaut. Their lives will consist mostly of ordinary days, and even some disappointing ones. Bills and laundry will pile up. There will be Black Mondays on the stock market. Relationships will go sour. And even now, seeing how hard it is for our kids just to share their toys and to learn to stop interrupting, we are often painfully aware that their human flaws—the unappealing traits that mar the perfection of their newborn selves—will be with them all their lives, just as our own flaws remain with us. "Things fall apart," wrote Yeats. "The center cannot hold."

And so we wonder: Can even a trace of their precious trust and innocence be preserved as our children grow toward adulthood? We yearn to offer them something that will enable them to hold on to that inner beauty, something truly lasting, something we might call *spiritual.*

In *The Chosen*, the author Chaim Potok depicts a father's pained recollections of his early years with his son. The boy, Daniel, has "a mind like a jewel," recalls the father, and learns to read at the age of four.

"There was no soul in my four-year-old Daniel, there was only his mind," says the father. "Ah, what a curse it is, what an anguish it is to have a Daniel, whose mind is like a pearl, like a sun."

When little Daniel reads a book about a poor, suffering Jew, his father is shocked at his utter indifference to the character's miseries. The boy only bursts with pride at his own ability to recount the story from memory.

"He was a mind in a body without a soul," the father laments. "I went away and cried to the Master of the Universe, 'What have you done to me? A mind like this I need for a son? A *heart* I need for a son, a *soul* I need for a son, *compassion* I want from my son, righteousness, mercy, strength to suffer and carry pain, *that* I want from my son, not a mind without a soul!' "

In my own life as a professional child-development writer, I have written many articles and several books on topics such as age-appropriate toys, discipline, feeding, safety, and schooling. These are the down-to-earth challenges we face on the front lines of parenting. They are important ones, and often difficult. But they are not the *only* challenges.

Something More...

Our generation is hungry for information about child rearing. We have more facts and charts at our disposal than our parents or grandparents ever dreamed of. In order to equip our children to "make it in the real world," we offer countless age-appropriate toys and educational programs. But in our hearts we know they will face challenges and pain for which these things do not prepare them. They will not achieve every goal they set; they will fall in love and get hurt; they will learn that the world is often not a nice place. We know they can go to all the "right schools" and end up with an insider-trading conviction. Despite an abundance of resources, our nation and planet are still filled with people who have no homes to live in and no food to eat. If our children are not to turn cynical or bitter, or end up ("a mind without a soul") blotting out the pain with indifference, alcohol, or drugs, they need something more than self-fulfillment to give their lives purpose.

Once I drove my five-year-old son to a children's clothing store to buy a spring jacket. As we went through the red and blue jackets hanging on the boys' size-seven rack, it slowly dawned on me that every single one was emblazoned with the word "Winner" or "No. 1." We would all like our children to grow up to be "No. 1," to go to the best schools, to land a terrific job, to live happily ever after. But it is a commonplace that even the "winners" in our world suffer—not from material poverty, but from depression, abuse, and addiction that bespeak spiritual impoverishment. What happens to the hopes and dreams and wonder with which every child is born? Can it be that in working so hard to prepare them for their future roles in society, we are neglecting to offer a vision of their place in the universe?

I talked with one mother who struggled to define the "something" she yearned to share with her own children. "I use words like *respect,* and *beauty, fairness,* and *savoring life,* with my kids," she said hesitantly. "But I guess what I'm really talking about is *spiritual.*"

*T*he word *spiritual* is not an easy one to pin down. For each of us, its meaning reflects our personal experience, temperament, and religious upbringing. In these pages, the word *spiritual* is used to refer to an *awareness of our sacred connection with all of life.* Our spirituality is our opening to one another as whole human beings, each different and precious, and our exploring how we can truly learn to love. Day by day it is our learning reverence for our earth and its creatures. And in countless ways that are often nearly imperceptible to us, our spirituality is our drawing ever closer to the divine source of sustaining love we call God— the Love, as Dante wrote, that "moves the sun and the other stars."

Through *spiritual nurture,* we seek with our children to celebrate these myriad connections in the most ordinary acts of everyday family life, from meals to playtime to reading aloud and even to settling differences. Through spiritual nurture we are blessed with the opportunity to share with our children something more enduring than the hope of success or even happiness. "Sometimes you think you'd do anything to make them stay this sweet," said the mother of two curly-haired girls, ages four and six, as we watched them make mud pies in the backyard. But spiritual nurture is not about turning our children into Pollyannas by sheltering or protecting them. Nor is it about hiding them behind the false certainties or abstract doctrines many of us grew up learning in Sunday school.

Perhaps the most remarkable thing about the prophets and disciples who have come before us on this path in our Western spiritual traditions is that they were utterly ordinary people who faced real problems. They were not what most of us would call "winners." As we read the stories of Abraham and Ruth and Peter, we see them go hungry, wander in the wilderness, suffer betrayal by loved ones. But somehow they stick together, feed the hungry, and cross the desert. Through it all, they live in the trust that their lives *count*.

There's no denying that our children will need to learn skills—from reading to swimming to using computers—in preparation for their twenty-first-century lives. But if we offer them *only* skills and neglect the spiritual, we are merely attending to the details of living and neglecting the center of life. The process of discovering this spiritual center is defined in some cultures as nothing less than *learning to be human*.

Without spiritual awareness, our children's lives will be immeasurably the poorer. "We die," wrote Dag Hammarskjold, in *Markings*, "on the day when our lives cease to be illumined by the steady radiance, renewed daily, of a wonder, the source of which is beyond all reason."

Have you ever seen Saint-Exupéry's watercolor illustration captioned "The Little Prince on Asteroid B 612"? Alone on his planet, among the stars, stands the Little Prince next to an active volcano. Frail though he looks, and in the face of danger, his small figure emanates great wisdom, peace, and love.

The watercolor is a powerful image of the spiritual life. Like the Little Prince standing beside the volcano, our children will face turmoil, uncertainties, and disappointments as they move out into the wider world. We can't prevent this. But through spiritual nurture, we can help them discover a paradox: Only through their willingness to face the world in love, to "suffer and carry pain," in Potok's words, can they remain whole.

We nurture a child's spirituality because, if it slips away, he is likely to spend a lifetime searching for it. In *Modern Man in Search of a Soul* Carl Jung observed that among all his patients over the age of thirty-five, there was not a single one whose problem in the last resort was not a spiritual one. Albert Camus wrote that the whole life of a person is "the slow trek to recover the two or three simple images in whose presence the heart first moved." As loving parents, we are blessed with the opportunity to offer our children images that are truly sustaining, unlike the false gods they encounter among the television superheroes and video games.

The Little Prince sums it all up. "The men where you live," he observes, "raise five thousand roses in the same garden— and they do not find in it what they are looking for." What we are all looking for is the spiritual life. It is no less than every child's birthright.

To nurture a child's spirit is not to provide him or her with lessons on religion or morality. We don't *do* spiritual nurture by setting up a schedule of specific "activities." In all the great religious traditions, spiritual growth is understood as a *journey*. It is a path or a way along which each human being travels, not only in moments of ecstasy or enlightenment, but in the day-to-day struggle to come to terms with the world in which we live. For this reason, spiritual nurture, like parenting itself, is a *creative* process. It is a work of the imagination. We need not worry about having all the answers. We need only be willing to accompany our child as she takes her first steps along the spiritual path. We see her with God's eyes, to "embrace" her, in Martin Buber's word, as a unique creation whose worth is infinitely greater than the sum of her skills and knowledge. And we come to know ourselves as spiritual beings, to be willing to bring our own hearts to rest on that which is truly central.

And so, as we shall see, wisdom and love, and not "expert" information or religious precepts, are the most valuable gifts we bring to spiritual nurture. Without these, we can do no more than put forth ideas, which sound as empty as the ones we ourselves heard as children. They amount to the dry bones of religiosity, without a spiritual heart. They are like the activity of the businessman in *The Little Prince* who thinks he owns the stars. Instead of contemplating their wonder and infiniteness, he counts them, writes down the numbers on a piece of paper in a drawer, and locks it with a key. "It is entertaining," comments the Little Prince. "It is rather poetic. But it is of no great consequence."

In the following pages, wisdom speaks in the voices of the dozens of mothers and fathers who shared their insights, dilemmas, and practical advice with me in ongoing conversations over a period of two years. (I have concealed their identities in order to protect their privacy.) More often than not, I did not need to seek out people to interview; as I quietly made what felt at first like a solitary journey—poring over books on spirituality and theology long into the night after the children were in bed, watching out for my precious few opportunities for silent reflection—other parents seemed to discern that I was a fellow-traveler. I began to notice that conversations with friends, with the mothers and fathers of my children's playmates, or with friendly-looking mothers on park benches, no longer revolved around childhood diseases, toys, and schools. They took a spiritual turn. What a joy it was to discover that we shared so many of the same experiences, longings, and concerns.

The parents' observations in these pages have a down-to-earth quality, I think, that reflects their origins on the "front lines" of family life; we talked at kitchen tables, summer picnics, and playgrounds—the places where parents like you and me, not professional theologians, tend to congregate. In virtually every instance when I set up a formal interview, our conversation began the same way: "Well, I don't think I'm going to have much to tell you," the person would say with a shrug. "I don't know much about spiritual things." But once we had talked for

... The Journey Begins

a while, and she or he could let go of worrying about sounding "religious enough" and speak from the heart, each of them revealed a profound and often moving awareness of the spiritual nature of parenting.

As you will notice, these parents talked frankly about their conflicts and doubts. They reflected on their own religious training—repressive or dull, and occasionally enlightened. They felt alternately sustained by and frustrated with organized religion, and there were those who were pursuing spiritual nurture without religious affiliation. Many were carrying on some of the traditions of their own childhoods, experimenting with Native American and Eastern practice, and exploring the richness of their own faith traditions (Christian or Jewish, or a combination of both). All were seeking ways to deepen their families' spirituality through everyday experience: through play, in nature, with music and stories, in the rituals of home and community.

Each of the chapters that follow is divided into two sections. In the first, you will have an opportunity to reflect on parenting from a spiritual perspective.

You will explore the relationship between spirituality and religion, and between spirituality and everyday family life.

You will learn how your child's spirituality is likely to grow and change throughout the early childhood years.

You will discover how in the most ordinary moments of our crowded lives—at the breakfast table, on the way to the school-bus stop, or in the family room before it's time to start homework—we are offered opportunities for spiritual growth.

And you will find ways to offer loving, hopeful responses to your child's questions, with reassurance that we do not always need to know what to say. Far from it: as our children continually remind us, there is *mystery* at the heart of things. (Sometimes

Something More...

"I don't know" can be the beginning of our most fruitful dialogues.)

In the second section of each chapter, you will find practical suggestions to help you use this information to enrich your daily journey.

You'll find a variety of suggested approaches to family spiritual practice, or ways you and your child can deepen your spiritual awareness together. Please do not think of these as "activities" you frantically need to pursue in order to "encourage" your child to "become spiritual." Often less is more. As you will discover, many of the everyday rituals we ordinarily perform as a family are opportunities to grow spiritually. We need not necessarily *do* anything more, only be more fully attentive to what we are already doing (which may even mean clearing our schedules a bit). As Zen practitioners express it, before enlightenment, chop wood and carry water; after enlightenment, chop wood and carry water.

There is no reason to be concerned if not every one of these suggestions appeals to you. At first some may strike you as "too touchy-feely," or "too religious." With time and a willingness to experiment, you will adopt a few, discard others, and discover that you and your family are on a spiritual path of your own.

At the end of the book there is an annotated listing of inspirational children's books and recordings, from illustrated Bible stories to Native American legends to environmental sounds.

Finally, because spirituality eludes merely rational description, these pages are filled with prose, poetry, and short prayers drawn from our biblical traditions and with quotations from some of the great classics of children's literature (which seem to express spiritual truths in simple ways that touch the heart). I hope you will enjoy and perhaps be inspired to share some of them with your child in the years to come. For those days when family life seems to mire us in responsibilities and details, these can serve as reminders that there is always wonder in our midst. And after all, even though making the spiritual journey with a child can be bewildering and even arduous at times, it is always a labor of love.

In Reference to Her Children,
23. June, 1659 [excerpt]

When each of you shall in your nest
Among your young ones take your rest,
In chirping language, oft them tell,
You had a Dam that lov'd you well,
That did what could be done for young,
And nurst you up till you were strong,
And 'fore she once would let you fly,
She shew'd you joy and misery;
Taught what was good, and what was ill
What would save life, and what would kill?
Thus gone, amongst you I may live,
And dead, yet speak, and counsel give:
Farewel my birds, farewel adieu,
I happy am, if well with you.
                                    —Anne Bradstreet
                                    (New England Puritan
                                    and mother of eight)

✳   ✳   ✳

Something More . . .

And the little prince . . . went to look for a sprinkling-can of fresh water. So, he tended the flower.

Your spiritual journey with your child did not start with this book. It began the day you first felt his small fist clutch your index finger, and the moment you were startled by the love that poured from your heart at his cry. As you move forward on the journey, you are likely to discover yourself looking back over your shoulder at your own childhood religious experiences, and noticing conflicts and questions that may have been long hidden from sight. As you share in the experiences of the parents whose voices you hear in these pages, you may wish to begin making note of your own in a simple **journal**. Many of the parents I spoke with decided to do this as preparation for our interviews, saying it helped them sort out their own thoughts and remember their children's most intriguing remarks and difficult questions. In your journal you might find yourself recording:

- inspiring moments when you are suddenly aware of parenting as spiritual;
- ways you are exploring your own spirituality (through conversations with friends in a house of worship, on long walks, in silence or in prayer);
- frustrations and dilemmas you encounter in your explorations with your child;
- your child's most memorable remarks and puzzling questions (in this way, when you are unable to reply on the spot, you can tell your child, as I often do, "Let me write down that question and think about it and we'll talk about it again");

... The Journey Begins

- particularly helpful quotations and insights that you come across in your reading or conversations with friends or spouse;
- your own answers to the questions in subsequent chapters.

Keeping a journal does not have to be a major undertaking. Just have a notebook handy and jot down a few sentences every day or two before bedtime, or whenever inspiration strikes. Don't try to record endless specific details. A single day's entry might be no more than, "Kite flying on the beach together— wonderful!" For many people, it is helpful to think of a journal not as a momentous document but as a "friend" with whom you are involved in an ongoing dialogue. With time you will begin to speak with increasing openness and spontaneity.

How Can I Be a Spiritual Nurturer?

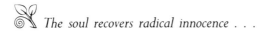 *The soul recovers radical innocence . . .*

—"A PRAYER FOR MY DAUGHTER,"
WILLIAM BUTLER YEATS

Most of us are astonished at the difficulty of simply getting through an ordinary day in the life of a parent. We spend more time than we ever imagined worrying about multiple vitamins, ear infections, and bowel movements. Living at the mercy of feeding schedules, day-care hours, and car pools, we do not seem to have time to contemplate lofty subjects. We probably don't think of ourselves as particularly "spiritual."

But we do remember that sometime, long ago, we decided that many of the things we learned as children about religion and God made very little sense.

What, then, do we have left to offer our children in the way of spiritual nurture?

Not surprisingly, we begin by reflecting on our *own* spirituality in simple, down-to-earth ways. With the help of other parents who have begun similar journeys, we pay attention to the challenging questions we may have been setting aside for some time. We recognize that questions and doubts are not stumbling blocks, but invitations to *growth*. What contributed to my own spiritual development as a child? What seemed to hinder it? Is there anything "spiritual" about my life as a parent? Is it hopelessly naive, in these unpredictable times, to be "spiritual"? How do I think about God? Are there rituals or observances from my own childhood I'd like to pass along to my kids? What do I want to avoid? Can involvement in a church or temple be meaningful for our family?

As we struggle to keep up with the daily routine—spooning out Amoxicillin, picking up toys, driving to soccer practice—there is reason to be grateful for these insistent inner questions. They remind us of our own small household's connections with people and traditions of the past. They call us to reexamine our place in the world around us. And they invite us to pause and reflect on what we can offer our children that is truly lasting. These questions draw us to the very heart of what it means to be a parent.

2. "But I'm Not Really Religious . . ."

"What is REAL?" asked the Rabbit one day, when they were lying side by side near the nursery fender, before Nana came to tidy the room. "Does it mean having things that buzz inside you and a stick-out handle?"

—*THE VELVETEEN RABBIT,*
MARGERY WILLIAMS

For many of us, being "spiritual" sounds a lot like having something unnaturally added onto our real selves, like things that buzz inside you and a stick-out handle. It sounds like being *religious.* And spiritual nurture, in turn, sounds like religious education.

Many parents have mixed feelings about this, to say the least. Part of the problem is that religion is equated, for many of us, with a set of relatively inflexible, rather improbable "beliefs" and rules, set down in dull, archaic-sounding creeds and dogmas. Little of it seems to have anything to do with life as we know it in the office, in the kitchen, or on the playground.

Something More...

It's easy to sympathize with one five-year-old Sunday school veteran who left his class with a long face. "All they talk about is God, God, God, God, God," he grumbled. "Why don't they talk about something *interesting*—like candy?"

We may sense that there is something missing from our lives and from the life of our child, but organized religion does not appear to fill the void. "I can't stand living like this anymore," said one woman who lives in an affluent New York suburb. "My seven-year-old son's friends all wear sixty-five-dollar sneakers. Their parents spend so much time traveling and working that I don't know how they ever find time to stop and hug their kids, or say I love you. All they're interested in is having an expensive foreign car in the driveway. There's no community anymore. There's no caring."

"You might find some community, or at least something more meaningful, in a house of worship," I ventured.

She answered without a pause: "But I'm not really religious. So what am I supposed to do?"

As we talked further, I learned that this woman had enrolled her two children in Sunday school, but she herself found church services uninspiring and did not really consider herself part of the congregation. Like many parents, she was "going to church for the kids," and finding little there in the way of spiritual sustenance for herself.

And there were a few parents who refused to follow that traditional pattern on the grounds of hypocrisy. "I'd like to go to church, but whenever I try, I sit there in the pew thinking I don't belong there," said another woman. "It seems to me that if I'm going to sit and listen to all that salvation and redemption stuff—and have my kids learn it—I ought to believe it. So I guess I'm neglecting my kids' spirits."

If in our minds we understand nurture to mean passing on religion, how can we offer it to our children when we're so filled with ambivalence? "I don't know what I believe, if anything, and I don't know how to answer half of my daughter's questions," said one mother. "I want to give her *something*, but I'm not sure what."

"I don't feel confident enough about my own image of God to be able to share it with anyone else," said the mother of two school-age boys. We reflect on the enormous problems facing our world and find it nearly impossible to answer the most basic questions: Who, or what, is God? Where is God? What is God doing? What can we honestly teach our children about God? What do the prayers and teachings we learned as children have to do with real life?

And yet many parents follow the traditional path of returning to church or synagogue after the birth of a child. Some of us do it out of sheer embarrassment on discovering that our child is utterly ignorant of the biblical personages and the rituals that filled our own early years. Childbirth, for me, had been a religious experience, but I did not instantly feel the urge to go back to church regularly. I did decide it was time to look into Sunday school when I asked our son, who was a talkative two-year-old at the time, if he knew who Jesus was, and he looked at me calmly and said, "*Jesus*—you say that when your car goes bump on the road."

Others of us return to organized religion because we would like to pass on some of the traditions and customs of our parents and grandparents. "My mother still shakes her head when she remembers how, when I was studying for my bat mitzvah, I told the rabbi I didn't believe in the parting of the Red Sea," said the mother of a five-year-old. This woman's parents visit Israel every year, and her brother has recently moved there. "And as far as I'm concerned, the whole idea of religion is that you just worry about following a lot of rules so you don't have to think about the *real* issues in life," she added heatedly. "I don't know what the spiritual part is, but I do think it's important to know who you *are*. For my son, being Jewish is part of his identity." The first time we talked, this woman had just, with some reluctance, enrolled her son in Hebrew school. "I signed him up because I don't want him blaming me later on for not giving him a religious background," she said, then drew herself up in her chair: "But enough is enough! I *certainly* hope he isn't going to be coming home after class and telling me I ought to keep a kosher kitchen."

I've talked with many parents, from a variety of religious backgrounds, who felt torn between the benefits they perceived in religion and the limits it seemed likely to impose. "I don't know," said a father of three boys as we talked over potato salad at a Fourth of July picnic. "I want my children to have the awareness that life is a gift—that we don't even have to *be* here, but we *are,* and that it's wonderful. But that doesn't mean I want them indoctrinated with ideas I don't feel comfortable about. I want my children to have the same freedom of choice when it comes to religion that I had when I was growing up."

When our children are taught religious concepts we have discarded, we discover that it is like rubbing salt in our own old wounds. I was determined not to expose my own children to the hellfire and damnation I had heard about during a brief stint in parochial school, back in the days of the Baltimore catechism. When my son was four, I signed him up for a week-long vacation Bible school whose curriculum featured nature walks, singing, and action-packed Bible stories. He seemed to love it. But one day, months later, he turned to me with somber eyes and intoned, "People who don't believe in God, when they die, go to a place where it's very, very hot and they *burn forever.*"

"Well, *some* people think that, but *we* don't," I snapped. "And *where* did you hear that, anyway?"

... "But I'm Not Really Religious . . ."

"At my vacation Bible school," he answered matter-of-factly. "The teacher told us."

Unfortunately, unpleasant surprises such as this are not uncommon. "Lots of other people seem to feel perfectly comfortable with this stuff," said one mother who decided to pull her child out of Sunday school because she considered the curriculum frightening. "I guess what it all comes down to is *I'm just not religious.*"

"I tried sending my children to Sunday school," another mother told me as we sipped tea at her kitchen table. "They came home saying things I don't want them even *hearing*—the same garbage I grew up with. So I didn't take them back." She sighed. "There must be another way to give my children a sense of the deeper meaning of life."

It would be foolish to suggest that most *adults* could mature spiritually without any attempt to understand the nature of the divine, or to learn from other people's spiritual insights and disciplines. The great religious traditions, properly interpreted, can help us do both. And many families discover that a faith community can provide a special quality of nurture.

But a number of religious educators point out that the *informed* choice of a mature religious faith cannot be made by a child. This is a decision he or she will make as an adult or late teen, most likely after some serious doubting during adolescence. Some parents find it helpful to consider a parallel with the child's future choice of a mate. In Western culture, we don't arrange the marriages of our children. What we do is to try to show them—by example, and in the context of their daily lives with us and with family and friends—how we struggle to sustain authentic, lasting relationships. Likewise, if we nurture a child's *spirituality* from an early age, we can trust that it will one day find expression and maturity in adult terms.

Something More...

There is an eighteenth-century Hebrew story about a young man who wanted to become a blacksmith. As rabbi Abraham Joshua Heschel tells it, the young man becomes an apprentice and soon learns all the techniques of the trade. He learns how to hold the tongs, smite the anvil, use the bellows. When he finishes his apprenticeship, he finds a place in the palace smithy. But all his skill at using the tools turns out to be of no use. He has never learned how to kindle a spark.

When a child's upbringing focuses merely on *learning religious symbols* rather than on *experiencing the spiritual reality* they (always imperfectly) describe, he is likely to reject them as hollow and meaningless upon reaching adulthood. He will have been trained in the techniques of the trade without learning how to kindle a spark. For this reason, one of the most helpful things we can do for ourselves and our children is to keep in mind the difference between *nurturing spiritual growth* and *passing on a religion.* Lighting candles, singing hymns, listening to the prayers and stories our parents and grandparents held sacred can evoke beauty and wonder. They can remind us of the presence and mystery of the divine.

But religious rituals and teaching are only meaningful when they point us toward the connections with all life, human and divine, which we have described as *spiritual.* Religion merely as a collection of precepts and rituals is lifeless. It amounts to nothing more than the things that buzz inside you and the stick-out handle, which (as the Velveteen Rabbit learned) are not the same as becoming "Real."

"My parents and Sunday school teachers talked a lot about love, love, love, but in a totally unloving way," said a father of three who was raised in a fundamentalist Christian home. "With my daughters, I think it's more important for them to know firsthand, through our genuine acceptance of who they are as people, what love really *is.*"

..."But I'm Not Really Religious . . ."

If we provide our children with the language of religion—with mere *descriptions* of spirituality—without offering to live it along with them, then what we are doing is something like providing a mouth-watering description of strawberry ice cream and then holding out an empty cone.

That is why, in these pages, you will have an opportunity to approach spiritual nurture from a fresh perspective. Rather than worrying about how to *tell* your child *about* God, you will discover how you and your child can *attend to* the divine presence in daily life. Somewhere along the way, you may notice that the language of religion has begun to sound more meaningful, maybe, or more personal. But for now, you need only open your heart. For a parent, the birth of a child is an invitation to go back to the beginning. It is an opportunity to accompany a child on a journey to the sacred places of life. It is a time to discover nothing less than the wondrous and truly awe-inspiring signs of the divine presence in our midst.

> *"Real isn't how you are made," said the Skin Horse. "It's a thing that happens to you. When a child loves you for a long, long time, not just to play with, but REALLY loves you, then you become Real."*

Spiritual nurture does not happen according to schedule, or by means of some mysterious formula. It is a process of gentle encouragement and patient waiting as the child's spirituality unfolds, like the petals of a flower. For this reason, spiritual nurture begins with the everyday care we give our children. It begins when we are ready and willing to explore the rich sources of spirituality that are present in our lives seven days a week. More often than not, it begins with one small step.

Something More...

I talked with one mother of a five-year-old whose exploration has taken her and her family in and out of church and back again. "At first I decided I would send Charlie to Sunday school so that he would have a cultural background in the Bible and all the holidays," she recalled. "I wanted him to 'experience the myths of the Christian religion'—at least I think that's how I put it at the time!"

She began by enrolling him in Sunday school in a nearby church where she found the curriculum, based on a prepackaged worksheet program, "harmless but dull. Charlie hated it. At some point I realized nothing was going to work *unless I felt it,*" she said. "We decided he'd be better off taking a walk in a wildlife sanctuary once a week." Mother and son spent many happy hours exploring the local park, picking berries and apples at nearby farms, and gardening together in the backyard.

But this mother found that she was eager to explore the connection between nature and spirituality more deeply. She also felt a need to join with other families engaged in a similar search. Happily, an adult discussion group on spirituality and ecology was forming at the same nearby church. Soon members of the group were revising the Sunday school curriculum to include hands-on encounters with natural materials, and visits to woodlands and streams. Now Charlie is a student in the third-grade class, and his mother is one of the teachers.

"The program still has problems. The curriculum emphasizes the hands-on aspect so much that God hardly ever gets mentioned, and lately I'm discovering I *like* God," she says with a smile. "I guess I'm still searching."

This mother is one of the many parents we will meet who have discovered that spiritual nurture is an often-unpredictable process. As we take the spiritual journey with our child, we need not be surprised or upset to discover that there are detours and dead ends along the road. Being a spiritual nurturer is not the same as *teaching* our kids something. When we teach, we draw confidence from our sense of mastery of the subject. We can check our first-grader's math homework, knowing we have had practice in adding and subtracting. When the subject is spiritual, most of us lack comparable confidence and practice.

We cannot expect to offer a vision of life free of doubts or uncertainties. We need not provide rapid-fire responses to the extraordinarily challenging questions they ask at the most awkward moments. Nor should we set ourselves up as paragons of virtue, raising starched goody-goodies.

But we do have something to *share*. What we can share are the sustaining moments in our lives when we become deeply aware of our own spirituality, our own connection with all of life. These are the moments we may find ourselves describing as "reverent" or "sacred" or "peaceful." These are our fleeting glimpses of a reality deeper than that which we can see and touch, instants when we sense that we belong to the land, the sky, to those around us, to life itself. We can never fully express them in words.

In the Bible, we read of a voice from the clouds or a burning bush, images that evoke the awe human beings have always felt in sensing the divine presence. For us, such a moment of aware-ness may come in nature—perhaps as we sit in an open field on a camping trip, and watch the dawn spread across the sky. We may recognize this spiritual connection when we are making love. Or, as we began by saying, we may discover it in the wonder and joy our children bring. Now, through our children's eyes, we have an opportunity to become visionaries, to see the world as a new creation.

"There's no question that everything is more amazing to me since Robert was born," said the mother of a four-year-old. "Every leaf, every bug that crawls along the sidewalk, is new and fascinating to him."

Something More . . .

To be willing to share in that wonder with our child, to help him or her continually rediscover it in the years to come—to enable him to keep in touch with life's blessings as he encounters life's pain—is to offer spiritual nurture.

How like an angel came I down!
How bright are all things here!
When first among his works I did appear
Oh, how their glory did me crown!
The world resembled his eternity,
In which my soul did walk;
And everything that I did see
Did with me talk . . .

A native health and innocence
Within my bones did grow,
And while my God did all his glories show,
I felt a vigour in my sense
That all was spirit: I within did flow
With seas of life like win;
I nothing in the world did know
But 'twas divine. . . .

—"Poems of Felicity,"
Thomas Traherne

* * *

...**"But I'm Not Really Religious . . ."**

"Does it happen all at once, like being wound up," he asked, "or bit by bit?" "It doesn't happen all at once," said the Skin Horse. "You become. It takes a long time."

Spiritual nurture, as we have said, does not happen "by the book"—not even by this one. It is a day-to-day process that grows out of each family's circumstances, interests, and temperaments, and it need not (and cannot) be forced. In this section you will find questions to help you make your own way along the path. If you, like many people, are unaccustomed to thinking of your everyday life in spiritual terms (*"Me,* spiritual?" asked one father), be prepared for some surprises.

The questions that follow will help you reflect on your own life as a spiritual journey, beginning in childhood. Recalling your earliest memories can help you uncover some of your deepest feelings about God and the sacred. You may even remember times when you felt the wonder, awe, and sense of oneness with the universe that are usually described as "religious" or "mystical" experiences.

These questions will also help you recall (if you haven't done so already) aspects of your childhood religious training you found dull or even disagreeable, which is helpful as you evaluate approaches to your child's spiritual nurture.

Finally, they may aid you in exploring wellsprings of spirituality in your life today.

Please keep in mind that this is not a quiz to be zipped through in one sitting. Reflecting on one's life as a spiritual journey is a process that unfolds slowly. Begin by considering one or two questions at a time. Set aside fifteen or twenty minutes, sit down in a comfortable place and close your eyes for a moment or two, and take a few deep breaths. As you read each question, try to *see* the memories in your mind's eye. Now write them down quickly, without censoring yourself or worrying about your "writing style." Finally, over the next few weeks—while you are on your way to work, or cooking dinner, or jogging—reflect on your responses. Be open to what your heart tells you. You are likely to discover that you have a much richer spiritual life to share with your child than you ever imagined.

As you read further, try to keep in mind your responses to these questions. As you and your child grow spiritually, many of your answers will change. Certain impressions grow more vivid or take on clearer meaning. After all, following a spiritual path is a process that lasts at least a lifetime!

Go back to your earliest memory. Picture yourself as a child, as young as ten, then six, then three—as far back as you can go. Let your mind rest there for a few moments until a memory comes up, and try to recall as many details of the scene as you can. You may have been sitting in a playpen, or drinking milk at the table, having a bath, or playing in the backyard. Try to remember the furniture in the room (right down to the curtains), or the way the sky looked and the grass smelled.

Now look over what you have written and reflect on how you *felt* during that scene. Did you feel secure and nurtured? Frightened? Joyous? Hurt? Can you see any connection between these early feelings and your current sense of God?

Can you remember a person from your childhood—a grandparent, teacher, or craftsperson, maybe—whose image still conjures up a sense of spiritual connectedness for you? He or she may have spoken of life experience in a way that touched you deeply, or simply shared a profound compassion or creativity. One woman remembered her grandmother sitting in the backyard sunlight with an apron full of pea pods in her lap, shelling them. A man pictured his mother nursing his baby sister. You may think of an uncle doing a carpentry project, or an aunt who brought you to visit people in a nursing home, or an art teacher quietly painting at an easel.

Sometimes, though, your memory may be of a figure who is judgmental or frightening—a mean teacher, or a very imposing religious leader. "You say *religion,* and right away I think of the nuns hitting my knuckles with a ruler," said one mother.

The musician and novelist Eugenia Zukerman, writing in *Theology Today,* shared her early recollection of sitting with her doll in front of the family television set when the program changed and "a figure appeared on the screen—a man, with streaming white hair and bushy eyebrows."

She remembered watching carefully. "A commanding presence. He stood on the podium, back to me; then, suddenly, he wheeled around, looked furious, placed a forbidden finger to his lips and hissed a loud and frightening *'Shhhh!'* " she recalled.

"I was the only one in the room. He must be talking to me, I thought. I was mesmerized. This man had power. This must be God, I reasoned. And there are those who say Toscanini would have agreed."

Realizing that we have a scary or distant picture of God in the back of our minds can help us understand why we often feel reluctant to talk about God with our children. "It was all guilt, guilt, guilt," said one mother. "Who'd want to visit *that* on a kid?" But as we begin to open up to other images and feelings about God and the authentic spirituality we are discovering in our lives as parents, we grow more willing to share.

What do you recall of your own formal religious training? Do you remember dull memorization of questions and answers from a catechism? Endless services? Teachers who talked about a God of love, yet were cold or angry? Frightening stories from the Bible, or of the Holocaust? When we examine our feelings about our own childhood encounters with organized religion, we can focus on the hurtful or discouraging patterns we hope to avoid passing on to our children. (If the repression was severe, we may find it helpful to do so with a therapist or member of the clergy.)

And we can begin to recollect the positive experiences and impressions from those early days that we would like—somehow—to share with our child. "There were always a lot of older women at our church who made great casseroles for the pot-luck suppers," said one woman. "I had an immediate, overwhelming feeling of continuity, and of being provided for."

"Every Christmas our church had what they call a 'love-feast,'" recalled a woman who had been raised as a Moravian. "There were beeswax candles trimmed in red, and everybody got a candle, and we would sing a song called 'Morning Star.' The church would smell wonderful, all trimmed with greens, and we'd eat special Moravian buns, and even the kids got to drink coffee—with lots of sugar in it, which was a big thing!"

"The emphasis on giving, on caring for others, has stayed with me even though I left the church years ago," said another woman. "Often it was a message delivered with a lot of guilt. But I'd like to find another way to share it with my kids."

Can you recall moments when, as a child or an adult, you felt a oneness with your surroundings—a sense of peace or awe, an awareness of your own small but significant place in the universe? You would probably not have been capable of describing it that way at the time, of course, and you may not have consciously thought about it for years. But can you remember how it felt? In *The Passionate Life*, Sam Keen wrote of his conversation with Willi Unsoeld, one of the American team that first climbed Mt. Everest. On the way down, Unsoeld stopped to admire the view and saw a small blue flower in the snow. "I don't know how to describe what happened," he said. "Everything opened up and flowed together and made some strange kind of sense. And I was at complete peace." These times of feeling totally calm, open, and part of everything around us are known by many different names, including *mystical, visionary,* or *unitive* experiences.

Such experiences can sound intimidating to those of us who have not scaled such heights—geographic or spiritual!—but they seem to be far more reachable than we may suspect. In 1975 Dr. Andrew Greeley reported in *The Sociology of the Paranormal* that *thirty-nine percent* of adults responding to a national survey indicated that they had had a mystical experience (according to Greeley's definition on the questionnaire). *Half* of these people had never mentioned the experience to anyone before the survey. Similar results have been reported by British and German studies. We need not be surprised, or consider ourselves "strange," if we recall similar encounters. One man I spoke to remembered the first time he heard a recording of Beethoven's Ninth Symphony, in his early twenties. "I was blown away," he said. "I think that experience taught me more about what's 'out there' than anything I ever heard in Sunday school."

"As a child and teenager and young adult, there were many times I had the experience of being—well, part of the cosmos. I can even remember one time I shared this with a dog!" remembered one woman. "The neighbor's dog and I were lying in the backyard on the grass, under the sky. He was on his back looking up and rolling around and having a good time, and I was on my back looking around, and I just thought how

Winky and I were appreciating the sky together, and that he and I and the sky and the flowers—there was a lovely flower garden in this yard—were all a part of it. There was a very nice sense of peace and belonging."

You may be able to recall having similar feelings on a family vacation, in a favorite room at your grandparents' house, while visiting your "secret hideout" in the backyard, or even when the music was especially lovely during a religious service. As adults, many people report similar moments of awareness while hiking outdoors or gardening; working with natural materials such as clay or wood; listening to music; floating on waves at the beach; helping out on a community service project; and birthing or "coaching" the birth of a baby.

Are there times in your life now when you feel especially aware of the interconnectedness and wonder of life— moments when you catch yourself thinking, "Ah, there is a God"? Not all spiritual experiences are the dramatic, time-stopping variety described above. Most of the time, God speaks in a whisper. "When I hear people talk about these amazing, incredible moments, I end up feeling out of it," one mother told me. "I'm not all that emotional. There have been times when I've felt close to God, but I don't think I'm part of the 'God squad.' "

Although many of us have heard the presence of God compared to a "light," it is important not to confuse God with a *lamp* that can be switched on and off. God is always with us. Only our *awareness* of God dims or brightens. Reflecting on some of the loveliest times we spend with our children, it is not difficult to think of glimpses of brightness.

"Sometimes, late at night, when my baby wakes up for a feeding, and it's just the two of us sitting there in the rocking chair in the dark, and I can hear her breathing, I have a sense of being wrapped up in love," said one mother. "It's as though the whole universe is cradling us, holding us."

"You feel it at the amazing, beautiful moments, like when you're breast-feeding or watching your child sleep, of course, but I remember feeling it right after my daughter was toilet trained," said another woman, grinning. "She'd just go into the bathroom by herself, sit down, and pee. Wow, I'd think, somehow nature really *works*!"

In the next chapter, we'll explore how, as we learn to deepen our awareness of the divine in the midst of everyday life—often at the most unlikely moments—we can begin to share it with our children.

3. Spiritual Nurture for the Here and Now

"I fixed my mind on a young Swiss girl," [said Fräulein Rottenmeier,] "expecting to see such a person appear as I had often read about—one who sprung up in the pure mountain air, so to speak; goes through life without touching the earth."

"I think," remarked Herr Sesemann, "that Swiss children touch the earth, if they move along, otherwise they would have wings instead of feet."

—*HEIDI*, JOHANNA SPYRI

When I ask parents what they hope to accomplish through spiritual nurture, their answers are remarkably similar. "I'd like my child to grow up to be a good person," they say. Or, "I want her to learn to think about somebody else besides herself." Most of us tend to imagine a "spiritual" child as the kind who contemplates nature, donates her allowance money to the Third World, and willingly shares toys with a sibling. Miraculous creatures though they are, our children are also flesh and blood. Transforming them into the visions of serenity and altruism we think of as truly "spiritual" sounds like an impossible dream. Most of us, after all, have enough trouble keeping their faces clean.

The trouble is, you and I have a natural tendency to think like Fräulein Rottenmeier. You remember the stern Frankfurt housekeeper who runs the Sesemann household in Johanna Spyri's classic story. When the Fräulein sends for a companion for young Klara (her employer's invalid daughter), the creature she is hoping to get sounds remarkably like our idea of a "spiritual" child. The Fräulein pictures a Swiss child "sprung up in the pure mountain air" who "goes through life without touching the earth"—someone utterly different, of course, from the irrepressible Heidi, who gets into all kinds of nineteenth-century mischief. To Fräulein Rottenmeier's dismay, Heidi squirrels away rolls of bread in her clothes closet for her blind grandmother. She smuggles home kittens in her pockets. And she befriends a ragged organ-grinder whose pet turtle crawls under the housekeeper's skirts. To Fräulein Rottenmeier, Heidi is a "barbarian." Why can't the child understand that she should be "good and noble" and do as she's told?

That's child rearing of the old school, of course, the kind parents of the nineties dismiss as repressive and overly strict—until we turn our thoughts to spiritual nurture.

That the "spiritual" child of our fantasies bears an uncanny resemblance to the little Swiss girl Fräulein Rottenmeier intended to employ is not too surprising, considering the way spirituality is often understood in our culture. Many of us grew up with the idea that the "spiritual" realm was a place apart from real life. Certain people—ministers, nuns, and rabbis, mostly—seemed to feel a connection with that heavenly dimension, where God sat on a throne surrounded by cherubim and seraphim plucking their harps. A person's "spirit" was a separate entity, like a shadow, or a Halloween ghost costume. Good people's spirits went up to heaven when they died. Bad people's spirits went the other way. The purpose of religious education was to help us get our "spiritual" bearings, mostly by learning to memorize commandments, prayers, doctrines, and Bible verses.

"When I was a child, we were almost neurotic about getting the angels' names and the saints' lives straight," recalled one mother who was raised a Roman Catholic. "It was like trying to arrange socks in a drawer. There was never any discussion about what the saints and angels were supposed to *mean*."

Certainly they meant less and less during our teens and twenties, as we began to see the gap that yawned between all the company of heaven and our down-to-earth selves. What help were tales of faithful prophets, or visions of celestial bliss, when our own lives consisted of mundane problems— clearing up our acne, getting into college, launching a career, affording a first house? God and religion were little more than abstract ideas, and if our "spirituality" depended on following their commands then we were not, apparently, "spiritual" people. The real world, with its enormous problems, had turned out to be a more complicated place than anyone had told us in Sunday school. Many of the parents I've spoken with had reached that conclusion—a few with bitterness, many with deep regret.

The truth is, most of us would love to be able, for our own sake as well as our children's, to hold on to our childhood image of God. Yet somehow, like a helium balloon that has slipped out of a child's hand at a street fair, it has an irresistible tendency to drift upward and out of sight.

Something More...

I talked with one woman who had grown up in a church-going family. With admiration she recalled the missionaries who regularly visited her church to speak of their work among the poor in Africa and Latin America. She also remembered feeling deeply nurtured by the closeness and caring of that church community. "They were all *wonderful* people," she said.

Why, then, I asked, did she turn off on religion as soon as she left her hometown for her freshman year at the state university?

"I wasn't turned off by it," she said quickly. "It just *did not apply*."

"I'm not rejecting a God, but I don't think about God a whole lot," echoed another woman, who runs a soup kitchen in upstate New York. "I think it's because my childhood version of God is no longer intellectually acceptable to me, and it's hard for me to feel I'm 'in communion' with someone—or some-*thing*—when I'm not sure what it is."

If the only "spirituality" we know is one founded on a belief in a life of virtue and a better hereafter, then we have a very hard time relating it to the world we know. Like Fräulein Rottenmeier, we are stuck with a view of the world that philosophers and theologians call "dualistic" because it divides our picture of reality into two absolutely separate dimensions: the "spiritual" world vaults high over the material one in which we live, like the heavenly frescoes on the Sistine Chapel's ceiling. The God we envision is always a Someone Up There, or The Man Upstairs. It is not easy to see a connection between that deity and the messiness, monotony, and struggle that, God knows, fill our days as mothers and fathers. "Are you going to include a chapter on the spiritual benefits of screaming at your kids?" one mother I interviewed asked me, only half-jokingly.

• • •

Realizing the emptiness of a "spirituality"—and of a "spiritual" nurture—that remains in the clouds need not bring us or our children to a dead end. It is a turning point. Now we can begin to deepen our awareness of the genuine spirituality of life's humblest moments. Authentic spiritual nurture is not the teaching of a collection of lofty ideals. It is not laboring to turn every moment of our family life into heavenly bliss.

We began by suggesting that spiritual nurture is a way of celebrating our sacred connections with all of life—with one another, with the earth and with God—in our *everyday family goings-on*. But for most of us, isn't home life measured in moments so utterly ordinary we hardly notice them, except to fret that we're not getting anything done? All those bottles, hours of rocking, nightly wake-ups. We'd just as soon forget all the diapers we've changed, all the hours spent patiently encouraging children as they sit on the potty, the number of public bathrooms we've visited. I'll never forget how startled I was, reading what I thought was a treatise on prayer by the fourteenth-century Englishwoman Julian of Norwich, and discovering that she recognized the workings of divinity even in human digestion: "A man walks upright," she wrote, "and the food in his body is shut in as if in a well-made purse. When the time of his necessity comes, the purse is opened and then shut again, in most seemly fashion. And it is God who does this, as it is shown when he says that he comes down to us in our humblest needs. For he does not despise what he has made." Julian had cast a new light on the humblest tasks of parenting.

A small elbow sends a cup of juice flying, and a toddler wipes up the spilled liquid with a paper towel until the kitchen floor is only slightly sticky. A bare-legged five-year-old makes his first broad-jump over a May puddle. Or, in the dark, an infant's startlingly strong lips find a nipple and latch on eagerly, and our gasp interrupts our own sleep and the night's silence. Rather than *interfering* with our spirituality, these are the ordinary miracles offered to us.

Spiritual nurture rests, as Willa Cather has written on the subject of miracles, not on voices or healing power coming from afar, but on our perceptions being made finer, so that for a moment our eyes can see and our ears can hear what is always around us.

A spiritual life is not something we begin to lead—or to cultivate in our children—after analyzing every book in the Bible, or resolving to be do-gooders, or even deciding we believe in God. Spirit is our life's breath. The word itself is derived from the Latin *spirare* (to "blow" or "breathe"), and the words most commonly used to denote spirit in the Bible—the Hebrew *ruach* and the Greek *pneuma*—are also the words for "wind" and "breath": the life-giving element within and all around us. The ancient Hebrews understood their own breath to be the breath of God. And the words for "spirit" in both Sanskrit and Japanese also refer to breathing; spirit is the breath of the universe, a cosmic force pervading all existence.

Spirituality is not something we need to pump into our children, as though it were nitrous oxide at the dentist's. Like oxygen, it is freely available to each of us at every moment of life. Spirit is in every breath we draw; and so is spiritual nurture.

On her rosy face was an expression of peace and blessed trust that must have appealed to her grandfather, for he stood there a long, long time without moving or taking his eyes from the sleeping child.

. . . Spiritual Nurture for the Here and Now

"Watching Stevie chase a butterfly across a field, or bite into an apple, I can see that there is an innate spirituality, an embracing of life as a gift," mused one father of a six-year-old one afternoon, as he studied his son's school photograph, displayed on the piano in the living room. "I guess my main job is not to mess it up!"

By then we'd talked for a few hours, and as I got into my station wagon and headed home, I reflected on the wisdom in the man's words. It occurred to me that he had pinpointed the greatest challenge we all face as spiritual nurturers: to become attuned to the young child's authentic spirituality, which—unlike our own—is still such an integrated part of life. An infant draws its first breath spontaneously upon emerging from the mother's body. Children seem to take to spirituality just as naturally as they do to oxygen. They come to us "trailing clouds of glory," as Wordsworth wrote. Just as emotions and movement and cognition are inextricably bound up together for them—they express joy or surprise or sadness from head to toe—children's exuberant spirituality is reflected in everything they do. And as we grow willing to recognize this spirituality, the way the father of the six-year-old did, the child in turn is blessed with the capacity to deepen our understanding of what it is to be spiritual. A child shows us the extraordinary in the ordinary, just as the toddler standing on a chair at the kitchen sink slowly and deliberately pours water from one cup into another, as mindful as a Zen practitioner of the fulfillment to be found in a simple task.

We may not always welcome the child's revelations, of course, any more than the people of Israel welcomed the fire and smoke on Mount Sinai. They disturb our routine. My daughter stoops in the driveway to pick up a fallen leaf and trace its dry veins with her stubby index finger; I am thinking it is time to get to the supermarket. My son is asking too many questions again, just when I am trying to sort out the papers on my desk. Children are, as Alice Miller has remarked, "messengers from a world we once deeply knew, but we have long since forgotten." As we walk the spiritual path with them, they help us to remember.

Perhaps nowhere is this dynamic more charmingly illustrated than in Heidi's relationship with her grandfather. The Alm-Uncle is a seventy-year-old hermit, described by the village pastor as "alone and embittered toward God and man." After a dissolute youth and the death of his illegitimate son, Tobias, Heidi's father, the Alm-Uncle is ostracized by the people of his native Dorfli, and he retreats to a mountaintop (the "Alm"). "The people down there despise me and I despise them," he explains, "so it is better for both that we remain apart."

Then Heidi is unexpectedly brought to live with the Alm-Uncle. Grudgingly he makes room for the little girl in his rustic hut. He hammers together a wooden stool for her to sit on at meals. He makes her a bed in the hayloft. And before long, he even begins to show a little tenderness. With Heidi the Alm-Uncle shares his bread and toasted cheese, and the company of his goats and mountain air. And Heidi in turn shares with him—by sheer force of her own lively spirituality—the possibility of a life fully lived.

The curly-haired Heidi is no goody-goody. But she has an exuberant sense of the wonder of every moment, and a loving awareness of her connection with all creation, which make her a memorable illustration of childhood spirituality. Each mountain, Heidi knows, has a name of its own. Schwanli and Barli, the goats, are her friends. And the wind roaring in the fir trees beside the house is an occasion for rejoicing.

One night, as he often does, the Alm-Uncle climbs the ladder to the hayloft where she sleeps to watch her in the lamplight. Gazing at the expression of "peace and blessed trust" on her rosy face, he stands there for a long time without taking his eyes from her. Finally, he is moved to pray.

By the end of the story, Heidi, like many a nineteenth-century heroine, has gone from abandoned waif to happy member of society. But what is more remarkable is the transformation we see in the Alm-Uncle as he opens up to the life-giving energy that flows through his small granddaughter. Able at last to accept his own humanity and that of the gossipy villagers, he comes down from the mountaintop.

In our lives as parents, we discover, like the Alm-Uncle, that we are growing alongside our children. One father of an eighteen-month-old girl told me about a particular morning when he was trying to rush her to the day-care center. "Katie was dawdling, as usual, worrying about her doll and her backpack and saying bye-bye to the goldfish, and I was getting upset," he recalled. "I was trying to remember the advice I'd just read in an article about handling toddlers. Finally, I just picked Katie up and started marching toward the car. At the time she had a vocabulary of three words or so. And suddenly, as we walked down the front sidewalk, she pointed behind me and said in her little voice, 'Bird.'" The father smiled sheepishly. "There was a scarlet tanager perched on the dogwood near our front door. I got the message. We stopped and watched the bird."

More than any complicated religious doctrine we might try to teach our children—more than any charmingly illustrated children's Bible, or glittering Advent calendar—it is through our everyday relationship with them that we convey spirituality. As we share our reverence for the natural world, the simple joys of family life, our dependability, and our unconditional love, we show them the face of God. We let them know that they can *trust*. In Erik Erikson's biography of Gandhi, the psychoanalyst observed that Gandhi's mother helped him develop a "deep sense of communion with the unseen and silent" and added that "no doubt a certain basic religiosity—the undogmatic sense of being carried along by a demanding and yet trustworthy universe—was first personified for Moniya in his mother." As we shall see, loving parents convey that "undogmatic sense" in an infinite variety of simple, spontaneous ways.

We are not going to stop and look at every scarlet tanager that we pass, of course. Day care and car pools are always waiting. Then there are days when the basement is flooded and, instead of taking our kids berry picking as we'd promised, we have to find a bucket and bail out. That is why it is helpful to keep in mind that, like just about everything else concerned with children, spiritual nurture almost always happens in ways we least expect.

I can recall one evening when my children were four and two, and I decided to take them for a walk to see the sunset over the Hudson. I had in mind a mountaintop experience. What *they* really wanted to do, of course, was stop to examine every fire hydrant and storm sewer along the way. By the time we reached the lookout point, the sky was murky.

"Oh," said one child politely as we stared across the hills, "I think I see a little orange."

As we trudged home in the growing darkness, I was feeling rather foolish. But when we reached our driveway, my son gasped. "See the stars all over the sky, Laura?" he said to his sister, sweeping his short arms toward the heavens. "God is shining on us and all the people in the world."

Their two small faces turned toward the sky, and their eyes were a constellation of four shining stars. I was reminded, and not for the last time, that spiritual nurture is not a process of staging extraordinary experiences for our children, but one of enabling them to become more aware of their spiritual connection that is as natural to them as breathing.

> *Thou hast hid these things from the wise and prudent and rewarded them unto babes.*
>
> —*Luke 10:21*

*   *   *

. . . Heidi had gazed so often and so long at the lofty mountain tops that it seemed as if they all had faces and were gazing down quite familiarly at her, like good friends.

*T*he questions that follow can help us explore the spirituality in our daily lives and share it with our children. Rather than trying them all, choose one you find intriguing; each is likely to appeal to people of different temperaments and life experiences. Set aside a time when you are not likely to be disturbed (after the children are in bed, for example) and sit in a comfortable chair. Close your eyes and take a few deep breaths. Each time you exhale, relax. Let go of the tension of the day, and of any reluctance or nervousness you may feel about exploring the question you have chosen. Read the question and the comments that follow. Then ask yourself the question, and quickly write down all the responses that come to mind, without editing yourself. (If you prefer, just reflect without writing, but many people do find it helpful to be able to refer to their responses later on.)

Although questions such as these are often referred to as "exercises," do keep in mind that they are not spiritual aerobics designed to build you into a fit spiritual nurturer. As you will gradually discover, they help open your heart to God, from whom all nurture comes.

What does it mean to trust? Knowing that our child's spirituality is nurtured through his everyday trusting relationship with us, it can be helpful to reflect on our own childhood experiences of trust—and lack of trust. By recollecting times when we were aware of our ability to depend on others, or when we wished to be able to depend on someone else and were disappointed, we gain an understanding of the role of trust in our life and in our child's life.

Thinking back to your early childhood, picture the house or apartment you lived in. Remember your room, your bed, the people in your family. Are there times when you recall being able to depend on someone for love or reassurance when you needed it? (Did you run to your parents' room during a thunderstorm? Could you expect a hug and a Band-Aid when you scraped your knee? Was an older brother or sister around to protect you from a playground bully?) Let your mind rest on the memory long enough to *feel* the way you did when the event occurred.

Now pause for a moment or two. Breathe in and out slowly. Go back in your memory to times when you wanted to depend on someone but could not do so. Perhaps a parent or care giver was away from home, or too busy or ill to be able to understand or respond to your needs. Did you try and fail to express yourself? Take a few moments to recall how you *felt* at the time.

Continue this experience with later periods in your life . . . your school years . . . your years as a teenager . . . and up to the present. If you wish, record these memories in your journal.

Is God absent? "I think it would be wonderful if there were a God. I hope there *is* one," said a mother of two with a shrug. "But when I look at life as we live it, and what I read in the papers, I can't see what God has to do with it." Her words echoed the feelings of many parents I've spoken with.

Feeling the absence of God is not something that we need to try to ignore or overcome as spiritual nurturers. On the contrary, our willingness to face this seeming absence can be a new beginning. Letting go of contrived, lifeless images of God we may have acquired as children is a sign of growth. Feeling empty but willing to listen, we can trust that God will be revealed to us in unexpected ways, as spiritual guides have been reassuring pilgrims for centuries.

"Do not speak before God from knowledge," advised the sixth-century saint Isaak of Syria, "but approach him with childish thoughts and so walk before Him that you may be blessed with the fatherly care which fathers bestow upon their children."

Think back to some of your earliest childhood ideas about God. How did you picture God when you were five years old? Was God "an old man in pajamas," as one mother recalled? Was God a portrait of Jesus in your family's church? Did God seem kind, or very powerful, or frightening?

Now relax, take a few deep, even breaths, and focus on your current mental images of God. What do you think of when someone says "God"? Don't limit yourself to ideas of God you believe in. Simply let images of the divine float in your mind.

As you "see" each one, take a moment to hold it in your mind. If the image does not seem to represent God for you, allow yourself to let go of it with a slow, deep breath.

Who might God be? Many of us have heard the traditional names for God—*King, Lord, Father*—pronounced so often that they have long ceased to evoke anything about the nature of the divine. "Every time I hear a minister in church read the words 'The Lord says,' it reminds me of the booming voice of the Wizard of Oz," said one mother. "I get a mental picture of a small man hiding behind a curtain, running the show. No wonder I can't believe it!"

Recognizing that the traditional images of God have gone stale for us is an important step. Now we can begin to explore fresh ones that enrich our awareness of the divine rather than detracting from it. There is a Hindu practice of reciting the thousand names of God, as a reminder that no single word or image can ever truly comprehend the divine. "Words, any words, even the words of Scripture, are fingers that point to something else," writes William Johnston in the spiritual classic *Christian Zen*. "As long as we cling to words we will never have real vision."

Children, who are blessed with such imagination and curiosity, have a remarkable gift for suggesting fresh images. When I offered one two-year-old a crayon and asked her to draw a picture of God, she made a stick-figure of a pregnant woman. "I drawed a lady with a baby in her belly," she explained, apparently describing her ultimate image of nurture. Her drawing reminded me of a lovely verse in Psalm 131, likening God to a nursing mother: "I have calmed and quieted my soul, like a child quieted at its mother's breast; like a child that is quieted is my soul."

... Spiritual Nurture for the Here and Now

Exploring the feminine qualities of God may come easily, because in doing so we can draw on our daily experience as nurturing mothers and fathers—something most of us can't do by thinking of God as *King* or *Lord.* Rabbi Amy Eilberg, writing in *Moment* magazine, described the transformation of her own image of God during the first two weeks of caring for her newborn daughter. To her surprise, she found that the "tasks of caring for a newborn baby felt like acts of exquisite sanctity. The God that I had imagined [had an] understanding that my days had been filled with holiness, while I nursed the baby, rocked her, changed her and loved her." Now Eilberg began to feel she had a firsthand experience of God, rather than an abstract concept derived from others' accounts. "Once, God was only for other people—for Abraham, Isaac and Jacob, for Rabbi Akiba and Maimonides, for the men that filled the Judaism of my youth," she wrote. "Today, God is for me as well."

As we reclaim our spirituality by exploring images of God that we may not have considered before, we can begin to share them with our child on a more personal level. Take a few moments to examine some fresh images of God that may be meaningful to you.

Here are three simple ways to begin. Set aside ten minutes when you are not likely to be interrupted. Looking over your responses to the questions in this section and in the previous chapter, choose an image that resonates in your own heart, and let your mind rest on it as you close your eyes. Let your body relax, and breathe in and out slowly.

Recollect some of your loveliest moments holding your son or daughter. Now picture yourself as God's own child being nurtured and encouraged, bathed in love and warmth.

Or picture yourself floating in the sea which is God, rocking back and forth with gentle waves, holding you up and connecting you with the whole earth.

What are my life's miracles? Having a child helps us understand that the miraculous includes not only events that defy rational explanation, but even the most ordinary aspects of our everyday lives. No matter how many child-development charts we've read, those perfect fingers and tiny toes, the first tooth, the first word, and the first step are all more wondrous than we'd imagined. We can deepen that awareness by regularly taking a few moments to deliberately reflect on the miracles in our lives. As we notice God working when we least expect it, we discover we have much to share with our child.

One summer afternoon, I talked for a long time with the father of an eight-year-old girl. "Kelly *hates* her Sunday school classes," he admitted. "But I just don't know what else to offer her." He was disappointed, he said, that the classes did not appeal to her, because she was a generous, affectionate child who had what he defined as "a real spiritual side."

The problem, as this father saw it, was that the focus of the Sunday lessons seemed to be on church history and dogma. As we chatted, I asked him whether there was a time in his own life when he could remember being moved to an awareness that he would define as "spiritual."

His eyes softened. "There's a homeless woman I see in the train station every morning on my way to work," he said slowly. "She's dressed in rags, but she has the most beautiful singing voice I've ever heard. Her voice fills and echoes in the hall. Maybe I could bring my daughter to hear her."

What did he hope to convey to Kelly? I asked.

He paused. "It's a way of showing her that every human

being has something to offer. That life is a miracle. That we're all precious."

For this father, here was a first conscious step as a spiritual nurturer. Not surprisingly, it came to him at a moment when he stopped worrying about what his daughter should be *taught* and instead opened up to his own awareness of miracle. Although he later told me that sharing this awareness with his child was likely to provoke some challenging questions about poverty and injustice, he was willing to listen to the words being spoken in his own heart. Sharing miracles is not the same thing as having all the answers. Together we take one step at a time along the narrow path between glimmerings of revelation and profound mystery.

Set aside some quiet time to think of a miracle in your own life today. Did a three-year-old offer a playmate a lick of his ice-cream cone? Have the roses bloomed on the garden fence? Has a toddler's scraped knee healed? Did you and your child read a poem together, or hear some music, that touched your hearts? Think of a few such gifted moments you may have noticed in the past week.

Can I Know God?

One of our greatest gifts as human beings, and one of our most valuable sources of strength as spiritual nurturers, is the opportunity to set aside all our worries, responsibilities, and even doubts for a few moments each day. For many people, moments when we deliberately allow ourselves to feel rather than think about our spirituality can be opportunities to deepen our awareness.

A simple exercise in concentration is one way to begin. Choose a quiet time—preferably not after a heavy meal—and a calm place. (A bedroom is fine, although many parents retreat to a bathroom or even a closet!) Sit in a comfortable straight-backed chair. Now begin to notice your breathing. As you breathe in, feel the air filling your lungs and your abdomen expanding. As you exhale, feel the breath drawing out of your body. If you are distracted, there is no need to worry that you are not "doing it right." Take note of the distraction, set it aside for the moment, and resume concentrating on your breathing.

Do not worry that you are meant to be experiencing a "Presence"; just breathe. "Silence is the great revelation," said Lao-tse. Nor is there any need to think of this period of concentration as a marathon. Even setting aside only five minutes of silence each day can help our awareness move out of the head and into the heart, where we can begin to open up to divine presence. Later on in these pages, we shall explore some simple ways to share this silence with a child.

4. Hope to Grow On

 "And now," cried Max, "let the wild rumpus start!"

—*WHERE THE WILD THINGS ARE,*
MAURICE SENDAK

They whine piteously for bubble gum at the supermarket checkout. They pick up the precision telescope we get them for their birthday and brandish it like a gun. They are fascinated to learn all they can about rocks, shells, and woodland creatures—but when they walk along the sidewalk they also like to stomp on worms and ants. Dream of angels though we may, there are times when we can much more readily picture our child as the gleefully demonic Max in Maurice Sendak's *Where the Wild Things Are*. Max, you remember, is the child in a wolf suit who chases the family dog with a big fork.

And then there are the "wild things" they encounter in the world around them. Starting with the first broken graham cracker the toddler refuses to eat, or the first time the preschooler wails, "It's not *fair!*" our children discern that life is not all smiles and hugs from Mommy and Daddy. Isn't one of the first expressions we teach them "stranger danger"? And as time goes by, they catch bits and pieces of the morning news.

("*Who* got killed, Mommy?" a small voice asks, as I reach over—too late—to turn off the clock radio.) They begin to hear us speak in tense whispers about sicknesses called "cancer" and "AIDS." No wonder they are afraid of the dark.

Childhood, for all its wonder, is often painful. Think about teething. When my son was cutting his first tooth I begged the pediatrician for a remedy to relieve the pain, which had the child waking up night after night screaming. We had tried commercial gels, teething rings, aspirin substitutes—even a little scotch rubbed on the gums. Nothing worked.

The pediatrician looked thoughtful. "You know," he said slowly, rubbing his beard, "this is the first of many times in his life when your child is going to be utterly miserable—and you won't be able to do a thing about it."

*U*nfortunately, most of us in the Christian and Jewish traditions were brought up to understand life's dark side in moralistic terms. The purpose of "religious education" was to exhort us to measure up to impossibly high standards, and to suggest that all the pain in the world was somehow our own fault.

"All we ever heard about in church was how 'unworthy' and 'sinful' we were," said one mother, a former Roman Catholic, holding her plump nine-month-old daughter in her lap. "Looking down at this precious baby, with her joyful little pudgy face, I have a hard time with that. Does *she* need a savior to clean up her slimy little soul?"

"I was brought up with guilt, guilt, guilt," said one mother who was raised in a conservative Jewish home. "Why would anyone want to lay that incredible guilt trip on a kid?"

We don't want to inflict guilt or pain on our children. "I try to share with Sarah my feeling that there is *joy* in sharing our possessions with others," one mother of a four-year-old told me earnestly. She was speaking out against our culture's me-first ethic, and the joy she spoke of is real; to help a child discover it is to give a precious gift. But for the naturally egocentric child—which is to say, for *every* child—the joys of sharing are bound to come only after long practice in delaying gratification, and much struggle with fear of loss. When spiritual nurture is a well-meaning attempt to deny this reality, it is not really nurture at all. It is an attempt to teach her to conform to an idealistic model for human behavior. Instead of whispering to the heart of the child in the wolf suit, it tries to dress her up in sheep's clothing.

I am remembering two three-year-old boys waiting in a church hall before a Christmas pageant. They are wearing white cotton angel costumes. On their heads are halos of golden tinsel; on their backs, wings of filmy gauze.

They are twisting each other's arms to decide who gets to stand next to the door.

Sometimes we would do almost anything to shield our children from pain. One five-year-old boy, whose superhero worship extended to Batman, knights in armor, and major U.S. presidents, asked his mother, "Nobody would ever hurt a president, right, Mommy?"

She swallowed hard, remembering that she had been only a few years older than he was the day she heard about the assassination of John F. Kennedy in Dallas. "I said, 'Not usually,' and changed the subject," she recalls. "And looking down at those wide eyes of his, I wished with all my heart he would never have to hear the real truth."

The "real truth" should only be shared when a child is

emotionally and intellectually ready to grapple with it, of course. (*In chapter 9, you will find developmental guidelines to answering a child's questions on difficult topics, such as poverty, violence, death, racism, and innocent suffering.*) But sadly, if our attempts at spiritual nurture are *all* sweetness and light, we are leading a child along a path of cynicism and even despair.

In *Growing Up*, the newspaper columnist Russell Baker recalls the day he learned that his father had just died of diabetes. Only five years old, he tried to share his grief with a pious friend of the family:

> For the first time I thought seriously about God. Between sobs I told Bessie that if God could do things like this to people, then God was hateful and I had no more use for Him.
>
> Bessie told me about the peace of Heaven and the joy of being among the angels and the happiness of my father who was already there. This argument failed to quiet my rage.
>
> "God loves us all just like His own children," Bessie said.
>
> "If God loves me, why did He make my father die?"
>
> Bessie said I would understand someday, but she was only partly right. That afternoon, though I couldn't have phrased it this way then, I decided that God was a lot less interested in people than anybody in Morrisonville was willing to admit. That day I decided that God was not entirely to be trusted.

It is surprising how quickly our children perceive the inadequacy of a cosmic vision that is all peace and harmony. Cindy, the mother of nine-year-old Mike, has worked hard to support the two of them since her divorce. She remembered the day he had a play date with a wealthy friend whose home was furnished with antiques, Oriental rugs, and the latest electronic equipment. On the way home in the car he was crowing, "Wow, they're really *rich*!"

Quietly Cindy replied, "Money isn't everything, Mike."

"Get real, Mom," he shot back. "You know it *is*."

*J*ennie, a peace activist who often brought her seven-year-old son, Martin, to meetings and demonstrations, told a similar story. One Saturday morning she went into his room and sat on his bed. "We're going to a peace fair," she announced, "with puppet shows, and guitarists, and food from all over the world!"

Martin, his head on the pillow, sighed and stared up at the ceiling. "Peace?" he repeated. "Peace? There will never be peace in every country in the world. Look at all the wars we've had! First we had the Civil War, then the Revolutionary War . . ."

He sat up and glared at Jennie accusingly. Martin's understanding of the past may have been a bit confused, but he had already developed some historical perspective.

Listening to Jennie's story, I was reminded of the observations of another child who eloquently expressed her experience of the chasm between real and ideal in her tragically short life. "It's twice as hard for us young ones to hold our ground, and maintain our opinions, in a time when all ideals are being shattered and destroyed, when people are showing their worst side, and do not know whether to believe in truth and right and God," wrote Anne Frank in her diary. "It's really a wonder that I haven't dropped all my ideals. In spite of everything I still believe that people are really good at heart." Remembering these poignant words, the novelist and essayist Anne Roiphe has observed that they are often included in seder readings, as a tribute to one young girl's determination to cling to truth and right in the face of unspeakable evil; yet only a few months after setting them on paper, Anne Frank was sent to a Nazi death camp.

If we are to offer our children sustaining hope, then somehow "truth and right" need to connect with life as we really know it—and as our children are coming to know it. We must help them face the realization that people can be both good and less than good at heart, and that life is full of suffering as well as beauty. Many of us who came of age during the decades when assassinations, Vietnam atrocities, and political corruption filled the news know only too well how empty simplistic formulas sound in the face of tragedy. "This generation thinks . . . that nothing faithful, vulnerable, fragile, can be durable or have any true power," wrote Saul Bellow in *Herzog*. "Death waits for these things as a cement floor waits for a dropping light bulb."

"I *envy* people who have faith," said one woman I spoke with. (I'll call her Eva.) As we talked at her kitchen table, her two boys' laughing voices carried up from the playroom. "But I grew up with the Hebrew stories of God's direct intervention in human behavior—the flood, the plagues, the manna from heaven. My own image of God is pretty much of a puppeteer up in the sky. You know the illustration on the jacket of the original Broadway soundtrack of *My Fair Lady,* with Henry Higgins manipulating Eliza Doolittle as though she were a puppet?"

Eva sighed. "*That* God seems like nothing but wishful thinking."

She gazed into her teacup in silence for a few moments, and when she spoke again her words came more softly. "I was watching the TV news coverage of a Boeing 747 crash," she said. "They showed a nine-year-old boy lying in the wreckage. He was still holding on to a toy."

Eyes liquid, she got up from the table and walked over to the sink. "I don't know how a God could let that happen," she said, staring out the window at the two small bicycles parked in the driveway. "I think if there *is* a God, his power must be limited to making nice days and pretty flowers."

It's hard to find hope in a God of nice days and pretty flowers in a world where there are also earthquakes and hurricanes. Paradoxically, real hope begins with the ups and downs of the everyday life we share with our children, and with finding God in the midst of the pain and hurt we cannot explain away. It is founded on the acknowledgment that the sun sets on both good and bad each night. Authentic spiritual nurture grows out of our willingness to grapple with our own doubts and anger, not our attempts to gloss over them. This is an insight that finds expression in the great spiritual traditions. More than two thousand years ago, the Buddha put it in a nutshell: "Life is suffering." Like Max, we and our children are invited to stare our monsters in the face.

One father told me how he surprised himself one morning when his two preschool girls were fighting over a box of crayons. "Why can't you share?" he demanded. Four-year-old Catherine looked up at him indignantly. "I don't *like* sharing!" she said. Her father stopped short. "I was about to say something like, 'Well, too bad!' " he recalled, "and then I caught myself. 'You know, Catherine,' I said, '*neither do I.*' She looked startled. And then, of course, she shared the crayons."

The *acknowledgment* of pain and the *assurance* of guiding love: this dynamic is the heart of spiritual nurture in our biblical traditions. It is to recognize the darkness in ourselves and in our world, and to know that we can still go on. It is to enable our children to confront their shortcomings in the knowledge that they are loved. It is to know that the suffering and tragedy in our world are real, but they are not the last word. It is the basis of hope. With each passing day our children are bound to make mistakes, to run into danger—to make "mischief of one kind and another," like Max. But that will not be the end of the story.

It is hard to think of a more inspiring embodiment of that kind of hope than Ruby Bridges, the six-year-old black child about whom Robert Coles has written often and eloquently, who initiated school desegregation in New Orleans in the face of heckling mobs and racial slurs.

Coles, having heard that Ruby actually *prays* for the mobs that turn out against her, asks her why. "I'm sure God knows what's happening," answers the little girl. "He's got a lot to worry about; but there is bad trouble here, and He can't help but notice. He may not rush to do anything, not right away. But there will come a day, like you hear in church."

Not every child will endure Ruby's hardships, and precious few of us show her courage at any age. But at one time or another, each of our children will know something of life's pain. To offer spiritual nurture is to help prepare them, not by denying the pain in ourselves or our world, but by letting them know that, like Max—who smells good things to eat and sails home to find his supper on the table—they can always find reason to hope.

✳   ✳   ✳

. . . Hope to Grow On

*Then all around from far away across the
world he smelled good things to eat
so he gave up being king of where the wild
things are.*

*W*e began this chapter by saying that spiritual nurture is not
a method of producing the perfect child. We don't want to
"lay a guilt trip" on our kids. We don't want spiritual nurture
to *add* to their pain. But there is something profoundly hu-
manizing about helping them to *face* it, even when we can offer
no advice or explanations. We can guide them as they discover
that they and their world are a "mixed bag," with many good
qualities and some not-so-good ones. He made his bed without
being asked this morning, but he poured orange juice into his
sister's Cheerios. Our town has some wonderful playgrounds,
but we saw a homeless man yesterday on Main Street. No matter
how many toys we have, be they a child's superhero figures or
an adult's stereo components, we always seem to want more.

Children learn these lessons one day at a time, through
years of temper tantrums, hard questions, and fear of the dark.
Our ability to help them, and to offer hope, grows out of our
own experience. For this reason, it is worthwhile to look back
on encounters with pain in our own lives. Begin when you are
not likely to be disturbed for twenty minutes. Find a comfortable
chair, take a few deep, even breaths, and let your body relax.

**Can you recall experiences of pain from your child-
hood?** Think back as far as you can, as young as five or three
years of age. Picture in your mind a time when you suffered a

physical trauma (from falling off your bike, for example, or tumbling downstairs) or an emotional one (from being scolded, maybe, or having an "accident" in public). Let yourself rest in the experience for a few moments. How did you feel while it was happening? How did you feel afterward? Was there an adult who helped you out? What did he or she do?

Now move ahead a year or two and recall experiences of pain later in childhood. One man remembered how at the age of seven he had joined the other neighborhood boys in some daredevil bicycling on a street that always flooded on rainy days. "My mother told me not to do it," he said, "and I did. Of course, I fell in. My clothes were soaking wet, but I was too afraid to go home, so I stayed out for hours. When I finally did go home, she was very upset that I had been out so long. She didn't scold me—she just helped me get into dry, warm clothes."

The same man remembered his fear during the Cuban missile crisis, when he was nine years old. "The whole family watched the news reports on television," he said. "I was terrified. But around the dinner table we had long discussions about it. My parents tried to answer our questions—and they told us they were worried, too. Then we prayed together."

Can you recall experiences of forgiveness? Forgiveness is one of the most profound spiritual experiences life has to offer. Do you remember the biblical story of the brothers Jacob and Esau? Jacob is the younger brother who dresses in animal skins in order to deceive their blind father, Isaac, into thinking he is the hairy, firstborn Esau. After receiving his father's blessing—and Esau's inheritance—Jacob runs away.

Eventually, full of fear, Jacob returns to Esau, bringing along his wives, children, maids, and flocks as a gift.

But Esau wants no gift. The two brothers embrace, weeping.

Jacob, filled with gratitude, beautifully expresses the joy of forgiveness. "Truly to see your face," he tells Esau, "is like seeing the face of God, with such favor have you received me."

Can you remember a time when an experience of forgiveness moved you so deeply? Moments of both *forgiving* and *being forgiven* seem to touch us this way. Think of a simple thing, such as snapping at your spouse when you're tired after work, apologizing, and getting a much-needed hug. Perhaps you remember a time as a child, when you broke a glass and an adult swept it up without a rebuke.

In adult life forgiveness can also be part of coming to terms with pain we may have experienced in our own childhoods—the absence or loss of a parent, for example, or a lack of nurture and support, or the resolution of a long-standing rivalry with a brother or sister. It does not mean forgetting the pain or pretending it isn't there, but acknowledging it and trusting that we can go on. In our lives as parents, we have more opportunities than we might have ever imagined to forgive—or ask forgiveness from—our children as we all respond to the stresses of family life.

How do you teach your child to express pain, fear, and sadness? Most of us think that our children express these emotions far too often, of course! But providing the vocabulary they need to put their feelings into words is a way of helping to acquaint them with the anatomy of their own hearts—even the dark, unlovable spaces. That this is an ancient spiritual tradition is clear to anyone who has read the Psalms, whose juxtaposition of praise and lament makes them a virtual catalogue of human emotions.

Storytelling offers rich opportunities to explore the world of emotions. Choose one of the books in the appendix, or make up your own tale to suit a particular occasion. Leave it open-ended so that your child can help you tell it, and listen carefully to what she says. When one two-year-old girl looked upset as her brother went off to a friend's house to play, for example, her mother told her, "Once there was a little girl whose brother went on a play date, and she was left all by herself with her mommy. How do you think she felt?"

"Sad," replied the two-year-old.

"Yes, she felt sad—and lonely, too," echoed the mother. "But you know what happened? Later on, her brother came home, and gave her a *big* hug. And when she got a little bigger, she had her *own* play dates." In a loving context, the mother had supplied the words the child needed to express her feelings.

Five-year-old Sam was regularly caught hiding his young sister Lisa's favorite doll. Sometimes he would even hurl the doll down the stairs while Lisa chased after it in tears. One day Sam's mother sat him down, put her arm around him, and asked, "Do you know *why* you hate dolly so much?"

"Because she's stupid and ugly!" he yelled, lower lip jutting out.

Softly, as she stroked his hair, his mother replied, "No, Sam. You hate dolly because you sister pays so much attention to her. You're *jealous*. Everybody feels that way sometimes. But Lisa loves you so much."

Sam didn't reply. But the next time Lisa came into the kitchen clutching her bedraggled doll, something different happened. Instead of leaping up to grab it away, he stared accusingly at Lisa and said, "I hate dolly because I'm *jealous* of her because you love her more than me!"

And then, to the surprise of both Sam and his mother, Lisa sat her doll down on a kitchen chair, trotted over to her brother and gave him a hug. "No, I don't," she said tenderly. "I love *you*."

Sam's mother had helped her child confront his own pain

and held out to him hope and trust so that he could get through it.

Pretend play or role-playing with puppets, small figures, or blocks also offers opportunities to share feelings. A child who is less verbal may more easily express herself through art. Provide crayons, markers, pencil, or paint, and let her experiment. Once she is ready to show you her creation, encourage her to talk about it. "What *is* that?" is *not* a good opener. Try, "Gee, that yellow paint is bright," or (for a stick-figure drawing), "Oh, that person is standing up. Is he busy doing something?" Often a child will reveal a great deal about her feelings as she describes the drawing. "Yes, it's a beautiful yellow sun," she might reply. Or, as one little boy said, "Yes, it's a daddy and he's in Boston on a trip for his job and his little boy feels sad."

How do you respond when your child brings up a painful subject? When a child is upset, we want to offer comfort, to find something positive to say. When the subject—death, a friend's divorce, the problem of homelessness in our town, the nuclear threat—is upsetting or bewildering to us, we may even wish to change the subject. (Because we want so much to share a sense of life's beauty and purpose with our child, this is a special challenge for spiritual nurturers!)

Yet unless we are willing to confront these difficult questions, our children will conclude that we are indifferent—or that the *real* truth must be far too frightening for them to even imagine. We need not pretend to *explain* all suffering. But by listening carefully to our child's questions, we can offer reassurance and encouragement as she comes to terms with it. "*Why* did Bambi's mother die?" my three-year-old asked me one night at bedtime, and I was instantly consumed with guilt over having let her see the movie.

"She died because she got shot by a hunter," I said.

But Laura was not satisfied. "*Why,* Mommy? *Tell* me," she insisted.

After a few more false starts I understood that what she needed was not a logical explanation from me, but some reassurance and an opportunity to sort out her own feelings. "Bambi's mother died because she was a deer, and some people hunt deer," I said. "But *people* mommies don't usually die."

"No, they don't," she said firmly. "They're not deers." She was silent for a moment; she seemed to be thinking hard. "But *tell* me, Mommy," she demanded again, "why did Bambi's mother die?"

"She died because she was shot," I repeated. "I think Bambi felt sad, but he had Faline and Faline's mommy to take care of him."

"Yes, and his daddy, too," she said soberly. She repeated her question a half dozen times more, and each time I tried to offer a slightly different perspective on it, which she pondered and then phrased in her own words. She was especially interested in talking about how sad Bambi felt. Finally, she was ready to go to sleep, and I tucked her in.

Next morning at breakfast, she looked me straight in the eye. "Bambi's mother died," she said simply. I guessed she had an early inkling that much of life's pain remains a mystery.

Do you offer encouragement, not praise? *Praising* a child ("You're so good at math!" "You're so pretty!") is a way of putting a stamp of approval on her good performance. *Encouraging* a child ("You worked hard at cooperating with Eric this morning," or "You spent a long time on your homework") is addressing the *process* in which she is involved in learning to cope with her dark side. This is an important distinction, because it makes all the difference between trying to create the perfect child—which only serves to shame her as she inevitably fails to measure up—and offering our *real* child food for the arduous journey of life.

"In nature, in creation, imperfection is not a sign of the absence of God," writes the theologian Matthew Fox. "It is a sign that the ongoing creation is no easy thing. We all bear scars from this rugged process." We seek to foster the growth that comes as the child learns her limitations and discovers the sustaining life of the spirit. (God's "power is made perfect in weakness," wrote St. Paul.) Interestingly enough, in the Bible praise is reserved for God; human beings greet one another with peace and blessings for the journey of life.

Do you share hope for our world? It is undeniably difficult to discuss violence and suffering with our children. Facing these without hope is almost more than we can bear. "When I read about an earthquake that kills thousands of people, I have a hard time understanding where God fits in," said one father. "The idea of 'faith' seems like a joke." "Faith" is not something we can spoon-feed to our children, as though it were applesauce, with hopeful aphorisms. Rather than offering false optimism— or quickly changing the subject—when our children share their fears and questions, one of the most hopeful things we can do is be willing to *listen.*

One mother of two boys told me about a conversation they had on Martin Luther King's birthday. "They wanted to know who King was and why we were celebrating. I told them how, when I was growing up in the South, black people couldn't eat in the same restaurants we did," said the woman, who is white. "Then, I told them, some people realized this was wrong, and they sat down in white restaurants and marched in the streets until finally the laws were changed. This made a big impression on my kids, because they have black friends in school. But they wanted to know why so many black people are still poor. So we talked about how changes in laws aren't all it takes—how we need to work for housing and better education. And we talked about the word *racism.*"

This woman had begun by simply listening to her children. In down-to-earth language, she had described a painful reality and her own personal encounters with it. Then, and only then, had she held out authentic reason for hope by portraying the civil rights movement as an ongoing struggle, with some victories already gained and many yet to be won.

It is a vision of hope conveyed not through a single conversation but through years of willingness to be honest about the world as we see it, and to be willing to explore how we can help change it. That vision, and not pie-in-the sky idealism or a denial of reality, is the only vision of hope that I can share with my children. It is the vision that enables us to "hew out of the mountain of despair a stone of hope," as King said in his most famous speech. It is the understanding that we and our planet were created to live in justice and peace—a journey that is undeniably slow and often agonizing, with many detours and stops along the way. The story of the Exodus, the escape of the Jews from Egyptian slavery in the time of Moses, conveys this message vividly even to preschoolers. A generation passed before the Jews who had left Egypt finally reached the promised land. Often they wanted to turn back. They lost faith. They built a golden calf. But that wasn't the end of the story. In the next chapter, we shall look more closely at the biblical vision of hope for our world—and how a child finds her own place in it.

5. Not Alone:
The Role of Community

Wilbur didn't know what to do or which way to run. It seemed as though everybody was after him. "If this is what it's like to be free," he thought, "I believe I'd rather be penned up in my own yard."

—*CHARLOTTE'S WEB*, E. B. WHITE

One summer in Maine, our car got stuck in a ditch by the side of a road, just north of rural Lincolnville. In the space of ten minutes I counted two vans, three cars, and a pickup truck whose drivers stopped to offer help. "Why is everybody being so nice to us?" asked a small voice from the backseat.

You can tell we're from New York.

And as we sat there brushing the black flies from our arms and legs, I was struck by the paradox our children grow up with. How concerned we are to pass on our heritage of independence, of being able to do for onself! We convey the message even to babes in arms. Our infants must be the youngest in the world to be expected to sleep alone. If we are one of the mothers whose child, by the third day of nursery school, insists on clinging to our legs, we wonder how we've failed. There are scores of child-care manuals on my office bookshelves, and virtually every one of them devotes endless pages to the issue of "separation." To grow up, in our culture, is to leave home. It is to become "autonomous."

And yet what is one of the first discoveries we make when we become parents? We find out that—as far as time, energy, and emotional strength are concerned—we are far from autonomous. We need help. During pregnancy, as we begin shopping for baby clothes and furniture, we realize that our money is going as fast as our waistline. We are grateful when friends offer maternity clothes and hand-me-downs. After the child is born, we are exhausted from lack of sleep. We welcome the friend who offers to care for the baby for an hour or so while we nap. Later on, when our child is too sick to go to the sitter's and we need to go into work anyway, we find ourselves desperately phoning friends for the names of care givers who can come to the house.

"Every Friday night when I was a teenager," recalled one woman who grew up in Brooklyn, "I had to go to my grandmother's house to turn off her lights and stove, because she wasn't supposed to work on the Sabbath. Superstition and conformity—that's all it was to me. And everybody knew your business. I couldn't wait to get away from it." Now this woman lives with her husband and two sons in a secluded suburban neighborhood, with woods all around her house. "My husband works long hours," she says. "Being alone with my boys in the house, with very little support, I find I look back on the old neighborhood and realize it had its good points."

Independence may have looked good when we were students and young adults, but for parents it borders on burdensome. And after all, the problems we are coping with reveal

. . . Not Alone: The Role of Community

"independence" as an illusion. When the growers put Alar on the apples, didn't it end up in our children's cups of juice? When the drug dealers stand on our streets, aren't kids buying those small plastic bags? Like it or not, the events in the wider world land on our own doorstep, and we are ill equipped to cope with them individually. Like Wilbur, there are times when we think, "If this is what it's like to be free, I believe I'd rather be penned up in my own yard." And consequently any "spiritual nurture" based on solitary basking in the beauty of the universe, or turning into a "spiritual" nuclear family, is worse than irrelevant. It is a cheat.

To nurture a child's spirit, in a world of peer pressure, television superheroes, and war toys, can sound like an overwhelming task. It *is* overwhelming, if we seek to do it alone. Up to now we have talked about spiritual nurture as though it were something we might accomplish, with the help of a book, in the privacy of our own homes—somewhat like discipline or toilet training. But it is not, of course. Spiritual nurture, which by definition fosters our sacred connections with all of life, happens in *community*.

> *It was the best place to be, thought Wilbur, this warm delicious cellar with the garrulous geese, the changing seasons, the heat of the sun, the passage of swallows, the nearness of rats, the sameness of sheep, the love of spiders, the smell of manure, and the glory of everything.*

One day my five-year-old asked me to unbolt the training wheels from his bike, and we wheeled it over to the elementary-school playground around the corner. Outside the gymnasium door, there was a man in work clothes standing on a ladder, replacing light bulbs. I held the bike steady and my son got on, gripping the handlebars with all his might. Then, as he started pedaling, I held his shoulders lightly and ran alongside him. "Let go!" he shouted suddenly, and as he took off across the playground I cheered and clapped—and brushed away a few tears. Outside the gym, I saw that the man on the ladder was clapping and cheering, too. Without words, we were sharing an awareness that something special had happened to both of us, as we watched one small boy ride solo on two wheels. For a few brief moments, we had recognized ourselves as members of the extended human family.

For me, it was a fleeting glimpse of the vision of community at the heart of our biblical traditions. To be in community is to understand that we were created to live as an extended family. It is to understand that our individual stories are part of the collective story, that our actions today will affect the lives of our great-grandchildren and their families. To know ourselves in community is to know our roots, to look back and learn from humanity's past mistakes, and to move forward— however haltingly—together.

To be in community is not to be alike or to think alike. It is to understand our often bewildering daily lives as part of the unfolding of the larger story of life on our planet. It is to recognize, as we do when we are leafing through our old family albums, that somewhere among the flawed and often frustrating people we see in the pictures—the uncle who tells sick jokes at the dinner table, the cousin who never stops talking, the two brothers who haven't spoken to each other in years—we *belong*.

It is to see ourselves *not* as narrow members of an elite or chosen few, but among the ever-widening circles of family, faith community, town, nation, world, creation. Martin Luther King,

. . . Not Alone: The Role of Community

Jr., called this vision "the beloved community." In this chapter we shall focus on the three concentric circles of community that form the context for spiritual nurture: family, local faith community, and the extended human family.

> *He felt the warm milk inside his stomach.
> . . . He felt peaceful and happy and sleepy.
> This had been a tiring afternoon. It was still
> only about four o'clock but Wilbur was ready
> for bed.*
>
> *"I'm really too young to go out into the
> world alone," he thought as he lay down.*

Family is the first community our children know. At home, our children have their first encounters with life in community. To understand this is to realize that our culture's dominant image of the family—as a cozy retreat among sofa cushions, an emotional air-raid shelter of sorts, or a "haven in a heartless world," as Christopher Lasch ironically put it—has little to do with real-life family as community. Our families are not isolated oases from the world. Even our ability to afford a roof over our family's head depends on prevailing interest rates. We are, for the most part, mothers and fathers who struggle to balance the demands of job and home. In increasing numbers, we are single parents. Our children spend most of their waking hours not at our kitchen table, but at school and with other care givers. Like hardworking shopkeepers who live over the store, we are reminded daily that the pressures on our lives in the world "outside" are very much the same as the pressures on us at home.

Happily, our family's ability to provide spiritual nurture does not depend on our living up to some mythical ideal (despite all the warnings of the religious right). We are not Donna Reed and Alex. We need not expect to offer our children round-the-clock serenity and wisdom. We cannot expect to offer them a childhood without disappointments or loss. Sometimes we get angry with one another, or drive one another crazy. Sometimes we smolder with quiet resentment.

But a real family can function as a spiritually nurturing community in three basic ways. First, it is a *living embodiment* of the sacred connections by which we have defined the word *spiritual*. In the course of the everyday chores and celebrations that make up family life, our children come to understand what it means to have a place in a community, how it feels to value people more than things, what it is to be sustained by sacred bonds. We sort laundry together, we glue broken toys, we try to learn to settle our differences. Love and forgiveness are woven—however unevenly—into the fabric of daily life.

Second, family functions as a *community of memory*. "Tell us about when you and Daddy got married." "Did you hug me right away when I was born?" As we answer these questions, our children come to see their own lives in the context of the family story and to understand how that story fits in with events in the wider world. At the dinner table they hear the same stories again and again—of a grandparent's arrival on Ellis Island, of the great-grandfather who was the grandson of a slave, of the hardships of the Depression, of the great-aunt who died in the Holocaust, of the uncle who fought in Vietnam. These are the stories that tell us and our children who we are. They remind us that our own lives are rooted in the past, and that our actions will affect generations to come. And as our children grow, they discover the joy of sharing their own stories. "Remember the time we found the baby bird and put it in a box?" they ask, harking back to a spring day a year ago. "Remember how the bird flew away, Mom?"

...Not Alone: The Role of Community

Third, far from providing shelter from life "outside" the home, through family life we offer our children *perspective* on events in the wider world. As we carry a casserole to the home of a sick friend, or air our concerns about events in Eastern Europe at the dinner table, or read a bedtime story about a child of a different race, we are demonstrating our place in the extended human family.

> *"I am not entirely happy about my diet of flies and bugs, but it's the way I'm made. A spider has to pick up a living somehow or other, and I happen to be a trapper. I just naturally build a web and trap flies and other insects. My mother was a trapper before me. Her mother was a trapper before her. All our family have been trappers. Way back for thousands and thousands of years we spiders have been laying for flies and bugs.*

I began this book by describing how it grew out of ongoing dialogues with other mothers and fathers who shared a yearning to explore the spirituality of family life. These are parents from various religious traditions (though many are unaffiliated or irregular churchgoers), but there is much common ground. In conversations frequently punctuated by our children's interruptions, we share discoveries, questions, and doubts that arise as we reflect on our own lives and the events in the morning paper. We mull over the connections between our deepest concerns and the day-to-day decisions we make about our children's schooling, discipline, and privileges. And we do our share of commiserating!

Friendships such as these, which seem to develop spontaneously among "kindred spirits," can be enormously supportive and challenging. For those of us on the journey, they provide a context in which to share our children's spirituality as well as our own. How did we used to see things when we were kids? What have we now in the way of accumulated wisdom? How did *you* answer when your child asked why Grandpa died?

As we seek to translate our insights into daily practice, a spiritual friend can offer advice and fresh perspective. From a practical standpoint, we can exchange information on local resources—from interesting books to sensitive teachers to inspiring nature programs—that may foster our family's spiritual growth. We can compare notes on the latest blockbuster cartoon *before* we bring our kids to see it. And in moments when we let silence speak in our words we can, however haltingly, share some of what is in our hearts. In our culture, spiritual nurture can be a lonely path and even a hard one at times, and feeling that others are close beside us on the journey is a blessing.

Perhaps surprisingly, a spouse may not be this kind of spiritual friend. For many couples, the open sharing that characterizes deep spiritual friendship is not easily enjoyed in the context of the daily burdens and conflicts of family life. "My husband doesn't really want to hear about anything spiritual," said one woman. "He thinks we have enough trouble just getting through the day with our kids."

In an interfaith marriage, when one or both partners becomes a spiritual seeker, religious differences that once may have seemed irrelevant now need to be examined. "It took us four years to find any common ground," recalled a former Baptist whose husband was raised in a Jewish family. But even partners with similar religious upbringings discover that as adults they have different responses to their childhood experiences and different ways of sharing spirituality with their children.

...Not Alone: The Role of Community

"I guess my wife wasn't as burned out by the church as I was as a kid," remarked one father. "She still has something you might call faith. And now if I show the least bit of interest in anything religious, she's so happy that she blows it all out of proportion. So I try to keep it low-key."

"The far more common pattern is for one spouse to be somewhat threatened by, or at best distantly supportive of, the other's journey," writes the psychiatrist Gerald May in *Care of Mind, Care of Spirit*. "There may be respect for each other's pilgrimages, but often there is little in the way of full understanding."

Fortunately, a spiritual friendship with someone other than a spouse can become the basis of a home-based faith community for couples and children. We can plan simple gatherings and activities, from picnics to long walks to Sabbath meals. For many parents, groups such as these are less intimidating than a traditional house of worship, and an opportunity—even for husbands and wives of different backgrounds and at different stages along the spiritual journey—to grow together. Even for families who do choose to affiliate with a church or synagogue, the special intimacy and informality of a "house group" can be deeply sustaining.

Many parents do return to organized religion for their baby's baptism, bris, or naming ceremony, of course, but that step is often taken with quite a few reservations. "I'm suspicious of institutions," said one woman who, with her husband, wrote a "welcoming ceremony" for their baby and asked a clergy friend to lead it in his church. "I worry that when your religion is based on being in a particular church, you end up believing you're part of a special group that has unique access to truth. There's a danger that you stop thinking for yourself."

"I would like to join a synagogue, but I haven't found one

yet," said a mother of two boys. "I like the rabbi at the one near my house, but I don't feel comfortable with the congregation. I like the congregation in the next town, but the rabbi leaves me cold."

Unlike our Old World ancestors who lived in village or shtetl, we can *choose* a religious congregation. We shop. Are the sermons interesting? Is the music inspiring? Do we approve the Sunday school? Do we like the people? Too often the answer is no. The sermon has little bearing on our real lives. The rummage sales, potluck suppers, and continuing requests for money seem to make our days more hectic, not more "spiritual."

The clergy are often surprisingly unwelcoming to those of us who are testing the waters. The people, for all their church-going, do not seem to be especially holy. Perhaps what is most discouraging is that religious institutions often seem to reflect the dominant cultural values more than those they purport to espouse. "The place is a fashion show," complained one woman about her local congregation. "You wear your fur in the winter, your hat in the spring. What's the point of getting up early for *that*?"

These mothers echoed the comments of many parents who had found their return to organized religion disappointing or even alienating. I knew what they were talking about, since I had had several encounters of my own with churches where religion seemed to be nothing more than "going through the motions," not to mention sitting through excruciatingly dull sermons. Why bother? Eventually, we did find a church where we feel welcomed and challenged.

It is a small place, and the emphasis is on integrating the tenets of faith with daily life in the wider community. Many of the members of the congregation have returned to organized religion as adults, and hardly anyone seems to be there because going to church on Sunday is the respectable thing to do; in most of our social circles, it isn't.

Like many other parents I've spoken with, I've found a special quality about the interaction in this small community. In the discussion groups and Bible study classes and community projects, we can share our faltering attempts to attend to the essentials of life.

No church is perfect. Like any family, it can be frustrating and disappointing at times. But as we mark the births, marriages, and deaths of the members of our faith community, we feel the ties that bind us to one another—despite our differences—and to generations past and future. We struggle to understand what our tradition can teach us about the pressures and crises in our lives today. We work together. We try to be honest about where we're falling short. We learn about ourselves. We grow. Entering a house of worship does not—*should* not—mean abandoning our critical faculties. It does mean accepting the fact that a community of faith is a gathering of ordinary mortals who are "in process," like ourselves. "You're not joining a group of perfect people, for God's sake," commented one mother of three who had recently joined a synagogue. "You're joining the human race."

For many of us, just as each of our own families acts as a tiny community of memory, the faith community through its rituals and stories offers continuity in an uncertain world. Parents from many different traditions have pointed this out to me. "There are certain things about our tradition I disagree with," said a Jewish friend who keeps a kosher home. "Don't get me started about the sexist prayers! And no matter what my mother told me, I *know* God never 'said' we weren't supposed to eat shellfish. My kids will make these decisions for themselves when they get older. But for now, if my husband and I don't bring them up keeping these traditions—keeping kosher, learning the prayers and songs—what will they have? What does our culture offer? They'll never know *who they are*."

"I'm not sure what I believe," commented another woman who had recently joined a Presbyterian church, "and I suspect there will be times when I'll tell my daughter I disagree with something they've taught her in Sunday school—or at least that I'm not sure about it. The service means next to nothing to me at this point. But I want to be there in church, because I want my kids to grow up knowing there's more to life than what's on Saturday-morning television, and I want them to hear it from somebody besides me."

I spoke to a mother of three who had been brought up in a Jewish family, married a Protestant, and then spent years searching for a tradition in which they would both feel comfortable. They finally joined the Society of Friends (Quakers). "When I go to meeting and realize that the meeting room has been used since seventeen fifty-four, I get tears in my eyes," she said. For this woman, as for many others, the tradition provides a *vision* of the way the world was created to be (the "kingdom" or "rule" of God), and her family's own place in it. "Some people may think they can teach spiritual values at home, but if our children don't see them reinforced in a wider community—if we are the only family they know who are taught these things—societal forces are going to overwhelm them," she went on. "Through this community and this tradition, we get a spiritual path that shows us how to consider our responsibility to the wider human family and the earth. We get a sense of our place on the planet. Without getting grounded in a tradition this way, I think you just dabble around. You never get to anything that's really enriching."

One reason many of us are reluctant to join a particular

denomination is that it implies setting ourselves *apart* f.
as a chosen few. Admittedly, this often turns out to be
(we shall discuss some of the reasons for that in chapte.
such an understanding is ultimately a distortion of our   _al
heritage. Churches are not meant to be private clubs. In bringing
us together, passing on the stories of journeys past, and holding
up a vision of life as it was created to be, they can inspire and
enable us to reach out to others close to home and around the
planet.

> *"Why did you do all this for me?" he
> asked. "I don't deserve it. I've never done
> anything for you."*
>
> *"You have been my friend," replied
> Charlotte. "That itself is a tremendous thing. I
> wove my webs for you because I liked you."*

Four-year-old Stephen lives in a city with a large homeless
population. One evening before dinner, he bowed his head and
prayed, "Please, God, send food for the poor people, and send
people to give it to them." Stephen repeated those words while
saying grace every night at dinner for several months. Soon a
food pantry opened in a church in Stephen's neighborhood, and
Stephen and his father joined the volunteers who were bagging
donated groceries. After their first bagging session, Stephen's
prayer changed. "Dear God, thank you for the food pantry,"
he said, and he did the same every evening for months afterward.

To nurture our child's awareness of the world beyond his
family, friends, and church or temple is to help him grow up
knowing that he is part of the *extended human family*. It is a
process that begins with the events of our ordinary days, often

in response to our child's questions. At breakfast one Saturday, he asks about a photo on the front page of the newspaper, and we find ourselves reading the headlines together. We go to a street fair and hear music from the Caribbean or from Africa. We learn some Spanish phrases from *Sesame Street* and look for opportunities to practice them. We make Japanese paper kites. And through the projects and programs of our local faith community, whether home- or church-based, we enable our child to discover how God works through ordinary groups of people to help the needy in our town, nation, and world.

One caveat: As we seek to help our children understand their place in the extended human family, it is wise to remember that we are *celebrating* our sacred connections with others. We need not suggest that our child will be a "better" person, or that she will "make God happy," by reaching out. We need only encourage her to recognize that to be part of the world community—and to love others as children of God—is a gift. The desire to reach out then comes as a natural response, just as Charlotte weaves webs for Wilbur because she likes him.

❊ ❊ ❊

*"Joy! Aranea! Nellie!" he began.
"Welcome to the barn cellar. You have chosen
a hallowed doorway from which to string your
webs."*

*C*ommunity is not something we can manufacture for our children. Nor need we try. As children of God, we are all born with the awareness of our connections with others. Are young children afraid of touch, or of their own dependence? To grow spiritually is to become ever more deeply aware of the bonds that unite us as an extended human family. Like Charlotte's baby spiders, who are informed by Wilbur that they have "chosen a hallowed doorway," we need only recognize that. We need not waste our time in futile attempts to re-create the mythical small-town atmosphere of the "good old days," or in arranging the "ideal" environment for our children. To nurture a child's awareness of community is to strengthen his bonds with other people in the real world—people who may be different and even disappointing at times. In our culture, the word *community* is often used to refer to a rather closed-off static enclave (an exclusive suburb is "a lovely community"). But in biblical terms, to be "in community" is a dynamic state that reflects our underlying spiritual relatedness. For this reason, in this section we will not present a method of creating the "perfect" community, but a variety of ways to help us and our children deepen our sense of belonging within the family circle, in the faith community, and the wider world.

What makes our family a community? Through his daily interactions in the family, a child learns first-hand the meaning of love and forgiveness, acquires an early awareness of his place in a community of memory, and gains perspective on the wider world. To be spiritually nurturing parents, we need not be perfect people who never scream at our kids and never park them in front of the television set. Instead, we are ordinary mortals who struggle daily to discover the love that binds us together—a model for human community if there ever was one.

Reflecting on these questions is one way of deepening your awareness of how your family functions as a community. Choose a time when you are not likely to be interrupted for twenty minutes or so. Leafing through some old photograph albums or scrapbooks may jog your memory.

Looking back on my own childhood, what did I learn about community from my family life? How did extended family members, neighbors, or friends from church or synagogue provide support and continuity? How did my parents participate in community life? What problems did my parents face in the "outside" world that were reflected at home? What would I like to do the *same* with my own children? What do I hope to do differently?

What do I know about the lives of my grandparents and great-grandparents? About my spouse's ancestors? How and why did they come to the United States? What challenges and hardships did they face? What do I know about their daily lives—their homes, the food they ate, their moments of happiness, their disappointments? What do I know about the culture they came from—its crafts, traditions, language? What was important and dear to them?

Why did we decide to have a child? What is it we hope to pass on to our child? To have a child is an act of hope. It is to rediscover our own bonds with generations past, and to affirm our ties with those to come. As we all know, however, it is easy to lose sight of this dimension when we are bogged down in car pools and bake sales. For this reason, spending a few moments getting back in touch with our hopes and dreams for our child can be renewing. At first we are likely to think of our secret desire to see a son or daughter achieve something that reflects favorably on our genes and our parenting skills, like going to Harvard or winning the Nobel Prize. But as we reflect further, we begin to envision other things. What do we hope he will cling to as important in life? What kinds of relationships do we hope he will sustain? How do we hope he will remember us?

As a parent, when am I most aware of my own family as a small community? Backyard softball, dinnertime, raking leaves together, story time: Are these occasions when we feel especially close? When do I worry that our family is *not* in community? What problems (e.g., lack of time together, work pressures, too many extracurricular activities) seem to contribute to that? Is it difficult for me to feel we are in community when things are less than idyllic (when the kids are bickering, for example)?

How is our family sustained by the larger community? How do we reach out beyond our home? "There isn't much community," said one mother of two school-age children who commutes to a full-time job. Many parents I've spoken to regret their families' isolation and the lack of neighborhood life. Often our connections are made through school and PTA, Scouts, soccer, and Little League, service organizations, environmental groups, and church or temple.

In reflecting on your family's connections, ask yourself: In what ways do these relationships enrich our lives? How do they deepen our awareness of our connections with the wider world? How do they help us translate our understanding of these connections into day-to-day life?

Having reflected on our family life, with all its conflicts, pressures, and moments of bliss, we begin to discover that our family is growing as a real community. Here are some ways generations of parents have strengthened family ties.

Something More...

Remembering family history. Preserving and sharing our family's past is a vivid way of helping our child understand how community extends through history.

Keeping a photo album, drawing up a family tree, or compiling a scrapbook of "firsts" (a lock of hair from baby's first haircut, the first report card, and so on) are ways most of us naturally put together the pieces of our family story, and children are instinctively eager to look through them. If members of your extended families live far away, this is an opportunity to talk about them. Talk about your families' *names,* first and last. What do they mean? Why were they chosen? Can you remember any funny stories about your brothers and sisters from childhood? Where do they live now? Your children may enjoy helping you make a family tree.

Items from the past, whether they are family heirlooms, special holiday recipes, or mementoes of Coney Island visits, offer tangible links with the past. If your parents and grandparents were not collectors or pack rats, bring the kids to a local history museum and show them some of the items Grandma or Great-Grandpa used in childhood: apple peelers, coal stoves, washboards, pocket watches, and so on.

And grandparents' family stories—those tales we have heard so often we can tell them in our sleep—are a delight to young children. Even if an older person has difficulty remembering recent facts, he or she can often provide surprisingly detailed accounts of major life events. Suggest that your child ask Grandma about her wedding day, or her first day of school, or her first job. What was it like during the Depression? What was she doing on the day Pearl Harbor was bombed?

Setting aside family time. Setting aside time to do *nothing special* together offers us an opportunity to just "be" together, without chores or elaborate art projects to worry about. The idea of taking a rest from work is a time-honored one that dates at least as far back as the Jewish Sabbath. Be silly together. Let go. Put on the sound track from *The Little Mermaid* and dance together. Read aloud. Play musical instruments together (put a younger child on triangle, tambourine, or drum). Share a recreational activity you genuinely enjoy—chess, or touch football, or gardening, or baking.

Listening to one another. "There are times when I think, 'Get me *out* of here!' " said one mother of two boys. "These little guys drive me crazy sometimes. They're always up to something, and they never stop talking. But then I stop to really listen to what they say, and I realize that they're amazing." In our role as spiritual nurturers, we are apt to worry about what we ought to be *telling* our children about life and God. Yet *listening* to our children is at least as important as talking to them. By listening with open hearts, we affirm them as valued members of our family and enable ourselves to hear God speaking through them.

It would be foolish to suggest that we need to listen to *every* word they say, of course. There are times when we punctuate their chatter with regular nods as we try with little success to read the newspaper. But when we sense that the time has come to truly listen—when our child wants to share a problem in school, or talk about the salamander he found in the woods, or complain about a bad day on the soccer field, we are fully present. We make eye contact. We touch. We listen with all our senses, with our whole selves.

Expressing love. Our sacred bonds are affirmed in physical ways. A smile, a pat on the back, a love note or construction-paper heart slipped into the school lunchbox, a stroke of the hair, a hug, an "I love you" at bedtime—these are the ways we tell our child he is a unique creation and a precious member of our family community.

Each year around a child's birthday, many parents have a

tradition of sitting down and writing him or her a "love letter." Included may be a list of his most surprising and wonderful characteristics, a description of what he is learning in school, and some reflection on the challenges he is facing. The letter ends with some of the parents' hopes and dreams for their child's future. It can be saved and shared at some future date—confirmation, bar mitzvah, or high school graduation.

Trusting that every child is gifted. We tend to think of "gifted" children as elite with high IQs or extraordinary talent in music or art. But spiritual nurture is founded on the assumption that *each* human being has unique gifts to share with the community. One seems to be a "natural" with a soccer ball. His brother listens attentively to others and knows just when to offer a hug. Another child has learned three joke books by heart and is making up her own knee-slappers. Our world community is blessed by each presence.

Helping our children become aware of their gifts—not just because they are pleasing to us, or because they set them apart from the crowd, but because they are part of what makes them special, unique human beings—is one of our most important tasks as spiritual nurturers. As many spiritual guides have observed, a person needs to develop an ego before transcending it.

We do not need to sign up our child for a hectic schedule of classes and programs designed to promote his talents. Mostly we need to watch and wait. What does he seem to enjoy doing when left to his own devices? Perhaps he picks up the pencil we leave near the telephone. Tomorrow morning we can provide a red crayon. In a week, if he is still drawing, perhaps it is time for some poster paint. We are not thinking that one day he will be an artist; we are offering him the chance to explore the movement of color and the feeling of his hand against the paper.

. . . Not Alone: The Role of Community

He is discovering something about who he is, and one day—sooner than we think!—he will share himself with others.

Honoring the ties that bind us. One way we do this is by helping one another. Sharing household chores may sound like a doubtful path to spiritual growth. Yet what better way is there to demonstrate to our child that his contributions are important to the community?

Being responsible for personal tasks (bed making, brushing teeth at bedtime) as well as chores that contribute to the family as a whole (table setting, leaf raking) is not a way of "earning" their way into our family community, but a sign of their valued participation in it.

As parents, we also set *limits* on our child's behavior. Our ability to "control" them, or their willingness to "behave," are not the central issues, although spiritual nurturers face sibling rivalry, homework problems, and messy rooms as often as any parents. We have all read countless books and articles on discipline *techniques;* as spiritual nurturers, we are blessed with the opportunity to understand discipline as something deeper than technique. Discipline is an essential part of spiritual nurture because it is the way a child learns to honor his connections with the extended human family, with the earth, and with God. We seek not to "make" the child do things *our* way, but to guide him along the path of growth. That which breathes life into the techniques is our underlying attentiveness to the central task: to guide our children in the ways that help them deepen their spiritual bonds.

We seek to teach them to care, not merely to comply. When our children are young, we use only the usual simple directives ("Let's talk in indoor voices at the table, please"). We cannot explain all limit-setting; we may only say, "That's the rule!"

Something More...

But as our children reach school age, terms that are more openly spiritual begin to mean more. "Each person at this table has something special to say," for example. "Let's try to listen and find out what it is." These are lessons learned through years of repetition, of course! But the learning comes less from what we say than out of the child's own trust, the awareness that he is loved and cared for. And our ability to hold our ground—even when our child is unhappy about it—depends in large measure on our ability to view him in a larger, spiritual context. As M. Scott Peck has written in *The Road Less Traveled*, "the strength, energy and willingness to use these [discipline] techniques are provided by love."

Learning to cope with conflict. Spiritual nurture certainly does not promise an end to family bickering! But as we grow to trust in the sacred bonds among us, we can learn to settle our differences. Rather than splitting up our children when they get into arguments or shouting for quiet, sometimes letting them work through the conflict is a learning process.

For this reason, many parents find that a policy of benign neglect works best ("I don't get involved unless they draw blood," explained one mother). Sometimes, though, an adult can act as a catalyst, encouraging children to learn to resolve conflicts. With young children, for example, when a battle starts, one way to begin is by allowing each child (without interruption) to describe what happened from his or her point of view. "He sat on my Barbie!" "No, *she* knocked over my block castle!"

Next, we can help them suggest ways of solving the problem. "He should move his castle!" "She can play with Barbie on the coffee table instead of the floor."

Third, without trying to force an adult approach on them, we help them develop a concrete solution. "I'll move my castle if you play with Barbie over there." "Okay." Finally, there are claps and hugs to affirm all participants. This technique can be effective with children as young as three years of age. (*For additional information and approaches to conflict resolution at various ages, see the Resources for Further Exploration section in the appendix.*)

The World Peace Prayer

(from the Fellowship of Reconciliation, translated into more than forty languages)

> Lead me from death into life,
> from falsehood to truth;
> lead me from despair to hope,
> from fear to trust;
> lead me from hate to love,
> from war to peace.
> Let peace fill our heart, our world, our universe.

Attending to the sacred. In chapter 7 you will find a variety of simple ways to attend to the presence of God in the context of everyday family life. For now, here is a low-key ritual you may wish to try in your home. A major holiday, when children often expect and enjoy special observances, is a good day to start. Choose a time of day when your family is in the habit of spending relaxed time together: just before or after dinner, maybe, or at bedtime. If possible, be sure everyone in the family is home. You will need:

- a very brief, simple reading you would like to share—it might be a poem, children's book, or Bible story that you think your children will enjoy (see appendix for ideas) or that was a childhood favorite of yours. At a holiday time, an obvious choice is a related story or excerpt.

- a special snack to share (holiday or ethnic treats, for example)
- a candle, if you wish

Begin by quietly announcing that you would like to spend a few moments together. Gather in a room or outdoor area where everyone feels comfortable (some children prefer the living room or dining room, however, because it makes them feel grown-up and special). Say something like, "I would like us to have some family time to share a story (poem, etc.) that I really liked when I was your age."

If you are using a candle, allow one of the children to light it with your help, and suggest, "Let's all be quiet for a few seconds and just enjoy being here."

Once everyone has settled down a little, read the passage straight through. Do not explain it or elaborate on it (unless you need to define a difficult word).

Finally, you may wish to do some simple sharing. "This Thanksgiving, I am very thankful to have two beautiful children. Would anybody else like to tell us what he or she feels thankful for?" Surprisingly, the usual problem with this part is that it is hard to get children to *stop* talking. Once everyone has finished, allow a child to blow out the candle, and end the ritual simply ("Thank you, everybody. That was special"). Now it is time to share the snack.

As you and your family grow more comfortable with this ritual, you can adapt it to suit your own preferences and traditions as well as the time of year. One mother plays a recording of a favorite childhood hymn. Other families like to sing together, or hold hands while giving thanks. Several regularly read aloud letters from sponsored children overseas and then cooperatively write a letter to send back. (*For names and addresses of sponsoring organizations, see Resources for Further Exploration in the appendix.*)

How can we find a faith community we can feel part of? To join with other parents and children on the spiritual journey can be a source of mutual support and nurture. As we have discussed, this can happen in the context of family friendships that are sustained over time. Because in our mobile society relationships tend to develop in the context of our activities (PTA or work or school), rather than being carried on from our own childhoods, these friendships are unlikely to just happen; we need deliberately to seek them out.

Having met one or two fellow-travelers, we can all plan to do something together with our families. Depending on personal preferences and the ages of the children, hiking, helping out on a canned-food drive, or sharing informal meals together can be opportunities for meaningful conversation and simple fun. We share our day-to-day challenges and triumphs. We help one another out. In the long run what matters is not *what activities* we do, but *how we relate*.

Sometimes, particularly around holidays, parents decide to add some structure to these gatherings. "We get together with other families for a Shabbat dinner," said one woman whose family has not formally joined a synagogue. "We light candles, say the prayers, the whole thing. Sometimes we invite friends of other faiths to join us, share our traditions." Many families who *are* active members of a church or temple find a spiritual "home" in the more intimate small-group setting.

For practical reasons, small groups often do *not* include children, although they may be greatly sustaining to the process of spiritual nurture. A group of adults meets (usually on a weekly or biweekly basis) to share experiences, questions, and problems they have been facing since their last gathering. In one such group that my husband and I participated in, members arrived each week prepared to share their reactions to assigned readings—which were provocative works of contemporary theology. Often members read aloud a passage from the Bible and share how it relates to their own life experience. The gathering may end with a period of silence, or with some quiet music on the stereo.

By helping parents focus on their own growth and explore new material in an informal, nonthreatening atmosphere, small groups can offer a great deal of help on the journey. Social gatherings including children can supplement the adult meetings; these can include a potluck meal and a seasonal craft or activity for the kids. One group of families organized an Easter egg hunt for the neighbors and collected donations for a local food drive.

*P*articipating in a *house of worship* is more meaningful to our children if we become involved on some level, rather than simply dropping them off for Sunday school. Obviously, this means finding a place we ourselves can feel comfortable. "We go to a children's service that's just about as religious as I can stand," said one father of three boys. "The minister plays his guitar, and we sing a few simple hymns with the kids. They each give thanks for something that happened during the past week. Everybody gets communion, and we all go home."

As time goes by, we may wish to explore a little more deeply. We seek to discuss some of our questions, even share our doubts with people who, as one man put it, "feel closer to God than I do." If the prospect of attending weekly services is appealing, check your local newspaper for a house of worship sponsoring a lecture series on an interesting topic, or a reading group focusing on contemporary novels, or an "inquirer's class." Call the church or synagogue and find out whether nonmembers are welcome. Or just visit on a weekday and check the bulletin boards to see what kinds of activities and gatherings members are involved in—clothing drives, movie nights, prayer groups, day care or nursery school.

Many of the people I've spoken with expressed a desire to speak privately with a member of the clergy about their spiritual journey, but said they doubted the experience would prove to be fruitful. Many had been alienated by brief encounters with unsympathetic or uninspiring clergy during major rites of passage—their own wedding, for example, or a child's baptism. Several observed that the spirituality of family life was not something they had ever heard about in church, and they felt uncomfortable raising the question. Others worried about speaking frankly. "I could use some advice about spiritual things," said one woman who was raised a Roman Catholic, "but I find the priests in my local parish so narrow-minded that I don't think they believe there could be any merit to what I have to say. I guess I'm afraid of condemnation."

Clearly, there is no point in confiding in anyone who appears remote or judgmental. Ordination does not automatically confer the gifts of wisdom and discernment needed in spiritual guidance, and some clergy are more comfortable with this role than others. In the mainline Protestant churches, critics frequently allege that the clergy are hardly distinguishable from secular psychological counselors. Interest is growing, however, and if you do not find a willing ear in your local congregation, check with the spirituality department in a nearby seminary.

In seeking a spiritual guide, it may be helpful to ask ourselves whether our expectations are realistic. Even though we may not consider ourselves "religious," we tend to view members of the clergy as authority figures. Just as, in medical matters, our parents' generation took the advice of the family physician as Gospel truth, we expect the clergy to explain God and impersonate God as well.

Yet in very much the way we usually read up on childhood illnesses and learn to recognize our children's symptoms before consulting the pediatrician, we can measure a minister's or rabbi's observations against our own thoughts and the words we hear in our own hearts. A spiritual guide is a human being whose function is not to *tell* us who God is, but to enable us to open up to our own awareness. A compatible guide listens and speaks out of his or her own deep sense of God's presence, but our growth comes from the workings of the divine in our own hearts. No one can *give* us a spiritual connection with the divine; this is something each of us discovers for ourselves. Maybe it is helpful to recall an old saying: *God has no grandchildren.* Keeping this in mind, we are freed to approach conversations with the clergy in a more collaborative spirit.

What makes a *Sunday school* good or bad? "I would have been happy if they had read a Bible story and sung a few hymns," grumbled one mother of a four-year-old. "Instead they insist on using a dull packaged curriculum." No program is perfect, but the following are some questions to consider in choosing a Sunday school or religious school for your child:

• Are the teachers warm and loving toward the children? Do they appear to enjoy their work?
• Are the teachers trained to work with children? Do they have opportunities to share problems and information?

...Not Alone: The Role of Community

- Is each child's participation in the class affirmed, or is competition—who learns the most verses, etc.—the order of the day?
- Does the main underlying purpose of the program appear to be religious indoctrination (symbols, history, and hierarchy) or the children's spiritual development?
- Does the curriculum appear to be developmentally appropriate? Are children under the age of seven given plenty of hands-on materials? Are skits, artwork, and stories, rather than memorization of verses and historical facts, the basis of the curriculum? Are school-aged children encouraged to think critically?
- Are parents kept informed, through handouts, letters, or programs, about what the children are doing in each class so that you will be able to follow up at home?
- Are the religious practices of other faith communities treated with tolerance and respect?
- Does your child have a friend or schoolmate in the class?
- Are you comfortable with the nature of the material, bearing in mind that it is of necessity simplified for children?
- Is the school part of a house of worship you might feel comfortable joining?

How do we reach out to our extended human family?
Far more important than our ability to deliver sermons on peace and justice is our children's everyday experience in the contexts of family and our local faith community. Our child's view of the world reflects his own gradual development from an egocentric two-year-old into a social being who, by the age of seven or eight, can see life from others' points of view and begin to think abstractly about the social order. This growth reflects his everyday experiences within the family circle and, later on,

among peers and in the faith community. Caring about a homeless child, or wanting to give to those who have less than he has, will grow out of long years of learning to share, cooperate, and see things from someone else's perspective.

We can open our child's eyes to the wider world in many simple ways in the course of everyday life. We can offer opportunities for contacts with a diverse group of people (especially children). At the breakfast table, share an article in the newspaper about schools in India or life in a Brazilian village. Watch the Olympics together. Through library programs and school, encourage your child to get to know children of different ethnic, racial, and economic backgrounds and to appreciate how much we have in common. Many families find that a visit from a Fresh Air Fund child can be an enriching experience for their own children. Through Save the Children or another sponsorship organization, you might initiate a correspondence with a child in the Third World (*see Resources for Further Exploration in the appendix for agency names and addresses*).

The kitchen is a great place to "bring the world home" by preparing foods from different countries and talking about the people who eat them. Although many children object to anything "gloppy," they are often eager to try brightly colored tropical fruits. In *Helping Kids Care*, authors Camy Condon and James McGinnis suggest focusing on the ingredients in a Hershey bar—chocolate from Ghana, almonds from Brazil, sugar from the Dominican Republic, milk from Pennsylvania dairy farms, and corn syrup from Iowa cornfields, with the paper wrappers from Canadian lumber mills.

Helping a child recognize his ties with the heroes of history links him with the community of the past. Check the appendix for children's biographies of heroes from Abraham Lincoln to Susan B. Anthony to Rosa Parks. Children also enjoy visiting hands-on museums or historic sites where they can see demonstrations of life in the "olden days," learn about the hardships people faced, and discover what was important to them.

Joining the outreach efforts of their faith community and other neighborhood groups is a way many families find the support, expertise, and resources to visibly connect with the wider community. "That's why I became a Scout leader," said one mother whose son is eight. "Within a peer group situation, they talk about values like respect and caring, and they do things my son can understand, like running food drives."

One group of mothers I know brings their children for regular visits to see elderly people in a nursing home.

A father joined a car pool at his church to drive a disabled man to Sunday services. His two preschoolers rode along in the car. "At first they complained he was 'yucky,' " the father recalls, "but after a while, we ended up doing a few things together—we had dinner, we went to a baseball game, he made my daughter a doll—and they seemed to grow fond of him." A year later the man died, and the children still talk about him.

It is important to gauge a child's reactions to these experiences; there is no point in forcing contacts, or in frightening him. But as we make these connections with the wider world, we and our children discover that, in giving, we often seem to end up on the receiving end. "About once or twice a month I bring my five-year-old down to a shelter and we pick up a mother and child there and go out to a playground," said one mother. "To see the two kids going down the slide together, and to get to know someone who is facing life-and-death questions instead of worrying about which clown to hire for her child's birthday party—well, that's something that gets us out of our own rut. I'm not really sure how much our visits help the mother from the shelter, but they mean a lot to *me*." Each time we reach out to other people, we clear away some of our own busyness and see the world from a new perspective—which is another way of saying we seem to come a little closer to knowing God. Growth, as we so often discover along the spiritual journey, happens in unexpected ways.

Envisioning Community

Living in a fragmented world where we seem to spend our days rushing from one activity and appointment to another, sometimes we may have trouble envisioning community at all. This simple exercise in visualization for adults, adapted from Joanna Rogers Macy's "web of life," is one way of deepening our awareness of community. (Since it is not easy to read and visualize at the same time, why not ask your spouse or a friend to read this exercise aloud, and then trade places?)

Let your body relax. Become aware of your feet, your legs, stomach, neck, and face, and let them relax. Relax your arms and hands, let them rest comfortably. Breathe in slowly, feeling your stomach fill up with breath, then your chest, and visualizing your children who are breathing in with you . . .

Now exhale slowly, visualizing the warm air being expelled from your lungs, nose, and mouth, and mingling with your children's warm breath . . .

Inhale again, slowly feeling the cool air fill your nostrils, abdomen, and chest, and picture your spouse breathing in with you. As you slowly exhale, visualize your spouse breathing out with you . . .

Continue breathing slowly, in and out, and as you feel the breath fill your body, visualize your parents, your friends, the parents of your child's playmates, people in your neighborhood. . . . As you breathe out, picture your warm breath mingling with the breath of others still . . . the mayor of your town, the president of the school board, a checkout clerk at the local supermarket . . .

As you breathe in again, visualize others around the world who are inhaling with you . . . members of Congress, a hungry child in Mozambique, a mother in Latin America whose child has disappeared . . .

Now, if you wish, visualize the earth itself as a living, breathing being, pulsating with life forms . . . plants and animals, on land and sea, young and old, male and female . . . all breathing in and out, in and out . . .

Finally, picture the universe itself as the collective breath of God, filling you with peace, holding you in love, connecting you with all reality.

How Does My Child Grow Spiritually?

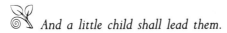 *And a little child shall lead them.*

—ISAIAH 11:6

*I*n some ways, spiritual growth resembles a game of leapfrog. As soon as we've got past one puzzling question, we discover we're faced with another one. For this reason, reflecting on our own spirituality, as we have been doing in the previous chapters, can be daunting if we believe that our child's spiritual growth depends on it.

Fortunately, our children's spiritual nurture does not hinge on our own ability to engage in discourses about God or to plan a hectic schedule of specially designed "activities." Spiritual nurture is a process of discovery, as we and our children grow to trust in and attend to our connections with God and creation in the course of our daily lives.

A child's spirit soars in the everyday pleasures of childhood. Playing let's-pretend, exploring the natural world, asking one question after another, sharing stories and music: these are the ways children celebrate their spiritual connections. As the child develops socially and intellectually, the process of discovery—and a parent's role as nurturer—changes, too.

6. As They Grow: The Spirituality of Early Childhood

"I thought Oz was a great Head," said Dorothy.
"And I thought Oz was a lovely Lady," said the Scarecrow.
"And I thought Oz was a terrible Beast," said the Tin Woodman.
"And I thought Oz was a Ball of Fire," exclaimed the Lion.

——*THE WONDERFUL WIZARD OF OZ*, L. FRANK BAUM

"I told my son that when people die, their spirits go into a new world. He understood that—or so I thought—because he'd seen cartoons about ghosts on television," said one mother of a six-year-old. "But then he asked me, 'If a spirit goes into a new world, does it have clothes on?'"

"I tried to tell Andy that God isn't a man—that we can think of God as a man or a woman," said the mother of a five-year-old, "and he wanted to know whether God has breasts or a penis."

No matter how carefully we try to speak to our children about God and spirituality, they seem to misinterpret us. Most of us can remember picturing God in highly physical, concrete terms. We had an image of God as a person, someone who probably resembled a grandparent or member of the clergy. And at some point—like Dorothy, the Scarecrow, the Tin Woodman, and the Lion—we can remember discovering that that image was a false one, and that we were not sure what to put in its place.

When I was five I knew God as a man on a cloud. I also knew that his angels came and sang to us every Sunday morning in church. During the sermons I squirmed in the pew, but afterward I could always hear the angels singing. Then one Sunday I discovered that the angels' music came out of the mouths of a group of grown-ups way up in the choir loft at the back of the church. After that, heaven seemed a long way off.

As spiritual nurturers, we want to offer our children something lasting, not stereotypes or cardboard characters which they will later discard in disappointment. We worry when we see them lap up miracle stories and rules ("You *have* to kneel down and point your hands up when you pray," one four-year-old advised her mother in a no-nonsense tone) which we know they are likely to call into question later on in life. We were hoping for a better way.

But we need not be surprised to discover that our children's grasp of religious concepts seems to be rather primitive. After all, their cognitive, motor, and social abilities are developing gradually all through the childhood years. Just as they may confuse *d* and *b* as they are learning to read, or take a spill or two the first few times they ride a two-wheeler, they are bound to pick up some childish ideas about God and spirituality. What we can do, just as we might with the reader or cyclist, is provide the motivation and skills they need to move on to a level that will offer more satisfaction and new opportunities to grow.

In this chapter we shall outline the development of these ideas in toddlers, preschoolers, and school-age children. But as

we shall see, *ideas* are only one element of childhood
Discussing religious concepts—*talking* to our child al
is only part of the picture. Spiritual nurture enco
whole child. It is inextricably bound up with he. ____
social, and physical development, and with her everyday experiences, beginning in infancy.

Educators have reflected on the process of spiritual nurture
for millennia, of course, and thinkers as diverse as Plato, Maria
Montessori, and Rudolph Steiner (founder of the Waldorf
schools) have offered observations and suggestions. Much of
our contemporary understanding of spiritual development in
children and adults is based on the pioneering work of Dr. James
Fowler, director of Emory University's Center for Faith Development, who has focused on understanding spiritual growth
in light of widely accepted theories of human development.
Drawing from his own extensive research as well as the observations of Jean Piaget, Erik Erikson, and Lawrence Kohlberg,
Fowler has defined a series of "stages of faith," each of which
represents a cognitive, social, and moral framework for an individual's approach to the transcendant. Since in these pages
we are defining spirituality as the awareness of our connections
to all life—to other creatures, and to God—each "faith stage"
amounts to a different way of knowing and growing in these
connections. As we shall see, spiritual development is an inter-
active process; as the child's inborn potential for relatedness
grows and develops, our everyday nurture—our chats at the
breakfast table, hugs at the school-bus stop, and stories at
bedtime—help it take root and blossom.

"How far is it to the Emerald City?" the
girl asked.

"I do not know," answered Boq, gravely,

Something More...

*"for I have never been there. . . . But it is a
long way to the Emerald City, and it will take
you many days. The country here is rich and
pleasant, but you must pass through rough and
dangerous places before you reach the end of
your journey."*

Just as it is a long way to the Emerald City, it is a long way
to the spiritual maturity of adulthood, and there is plenty of
confusion along the journey. But childhood spiritual growth,
like other aspects of development, progresses according to a
pattern. Do keep in mind, though, that this schema does not
represent a gradual ascent from a "lower" to a "higher" form
of spirituality. Each stage has wonders and challenges of its own.
And as spiritual guides have advised seekers for thousands of
years, to be closest to the love and wisdom of God is to be like
a child ("Out of the mouths of babes . . .").

The infant. Your baby's loud wail awakens you from a
deep sleep. You stumble over to the crib, gently lift her out
with a soft blanket, and carry her back to your own bed.
Supporting her head in the curve of your arm, you feel her
latch on and begin to rhythmically suck in your milk. You are
dozing lightly, enjoying her closeness and her baby smell.

This is a baby's spiritual nurture: food, rocking, skin-to-
skin contact. Her first "pre-images" of God have their origins
in infancy. Out of her total dependence grows a child's earliest
awareness of her spiritual connections, which Erik Erikson described as "trust born of care."

In the period from birth—and even before birth—to eighteen months, a baby is learning that she can be at home in the
world; she is acquiring what Fowler calls a ground sense of

hope, or "primal faith." During these tiring but exciting early months, we offer spiritual nurture in simple, physical ways. In the weeks before birth, the baby hears a familiar pattern of sounds: the mother's heartbeat and digestive tract, and even her parents' voices. After birth, she is picked up when she cries, fed when hungry, rocked to sleep. In the first few months she learns that care givers can understand and respond to her needs—for food or sleep, for playtime, or a change of scenery. She is discovering that when Mom or Dad disappears from the room they are only temporarily hidden from sight. She is learning that although sometimes she does feel afraid or hungry, she can rely on care givers to sustain her. When a care giver is absent for a brief period, the seven- or eight-month-old constructs what Dr. Daniel Stern of the Cornell Medical Center, author of *The Interpersonal World of the Infant*, calls an "evoked companion," or a reassuring sense that the care giver is with her even when not in the room. The evoked companion, Fowler suggests, may be related to the origins of her awareness of divine presence.

As she develops trust in others, the infant is also making discoveries about herself and her abilities. Some time between the second and eighth month, she acquires a sense of *self* as distinct from others and with the ability to act independently to some degree. She can bang a rattle. She can make objects move: roll a grape across the high-chair tray, flick a light switch up and down again and again. Now and for the first two years, the child is exploring the world through her *senses*.

Fowler calls the age of seven to nine months the "birth of the soul," which he defines as "the seat of emotion, intuition, and receptivity to God, and to others, deep within us." Now the baby, who can sit up and may creep, is relating to us and the world in many new and exciting ways.

She can share her *intentions*. She points to the cookie jar and says, "Uh! Uh!" With a clap and a smile she signals that it is time for a game of pat-a-cake.

She has learned patterns of familiarity and expectation which Fowler calls the beginnings of *ritualization*. She delights in a game of peek-a-boo, and goes crawling away at top speed, giggling, when Mom or Dad says, "I'm gonna getcha!" When we put her cereal bowl in front of her, she looks toward the drawer where the spoons are kept. When Dad puts on a jacket, she holds out her arms, inviting herself along on an outing.

The baby is also learning to share *feelings*. When she is presented with a new toy—or picks up a dangerous object (a pair of scissors, say)—she will look at a parent or care giver before deciding what to do with it. If the adult's face looks anxious, the baby will show the same expression and put down the toy or scissors.

Care givers, in turn, tune in to a baby's own feelings and help her express them. We smile in response to her gummy grin. We share her excitement over an autumn leaf that drifts by when we're out for a walk ("Look what a beautiful red leaf!" we might say, handing it to her). As we introduce her to her new world, she is learning that there is wonder and love in it. She is learning to *celebrate* with us. Some French and Swiss thinkers, Stern has written, observe that mothers express in these ways not only what they see their babies doing, but also their own *dreams* about who the baby is and will become. Through the simplest interactions, we begin to share a vision of our child as a unique and precious creation who is connected to all life.

The toddler. At around twenty-four months, as the child begins to speak in short sentences, Fowler marks a transition from "primal" faith to a stage he calls "intuitive-projective" faith. Now, and until the child is six or seven, her spirituality develops through *imagination* and *fantasy play*.

By twenty or thirty months she appears to have an image of God. This image is a projection of the loving care she has experienced (or, sadly, that she longs for). She is likely to be comfortable with an image of God "everywhere," or as an amorphous "spirit," because her own boundaries between self and others have not yet been established. "Thank you for the sun, God," one two-and-a-half-year-old was heard to say while playing on the driveway.

This period is also marked by the child's awareness of the forbidden. She gets into kitchen cabinets, climbs the furniture, pees on the grass. She needs, as we discussed in chapter 4, to learn limits from someone who sets them out of a desire to love and protect her. If she is reprimanded harshly, she will learn to "behave herself," but only at a great cost to her emerging sense of self. Even at this early age she will create a false self that will close her off from the gradual discovery of how her *whole* self—negative qualities and all—can grow to wholeness.

As we have said before, children do seem, on some level, to have an inborn awareness of their connections with others. Several researchers have pointed out that although we often hear how egocentric toddlers are, they can be surprisingly generous at times. The two-year-old offers a half-chewed cookie to the new baby, or runs to find a grown-up when a playmate trips and falls. We can nurture this gift by balancing our "No" with positive reinforcement. "Wasn't it nice when Janie gave Sam a bite of her cookie!" Perhaps most important, we can *model* these "prosocial behaviors." In our own conversations with our child we say please and thank you. We offer choices: "Which shoe would you like to put on first?" And in providing opportunities for her to participate in our activities, from stirring brownie batter to digging in the garden, we nurture her budding desire to cooperate and share.

"It seems to me that one way to understand faith is as the opposite of shame and the opposite of guilt," Fowler has observed. "Early childhood faith is a kind of robust sense of being held in the care and the love of God. It arises from the establishment of what some psychoanalytic theorists call a healthy narcissism, a healthy self-esteem, a healthy self-love, grounded in our experience of the love of others."

The preschooler. At three or four, the child is still in what Fowler defines as the "intuitive-projective" stage, and her enhanced linguistic ability enables her to ask more questions and develop highly imaginative understandings of the universe. The questions come one after another: "What's this? Who made it? Where did you get it? What do you use it for?" Finally—often out of sheer desperation—we end up saying, "God made it." So it is that our child hears of God as Creator. This, of course, only leads to more questions: "Why do people die?" "Why is God invisible?" "Who made God?" As we struggle to respond, it is helpful to keep in mind that her thinking has a magical quality until at least the age of six or seven. Although her questions may *appear* to be highly philosophical ("Why did God make trees?"), her thought process does not proceed in any recognizably logical way from one premise to the next. Instead, one idea follows another imaginatively.

"It's a good thing there's God, because if we didn't have God all there would be were dinosaurs and space," said one four-year-old. "And you wouldn't have a driveway to ride your bike."

By the age of four, children tend to blend together fragments of the stories and images offered by parents, preschool friends, storybooks, and television. Playing with blocks or dolls, they incorporate these elements into private fantasies. As they try to make sense of the world, unrelated images tend to collide and traditional stories get new twists. "First it was all dark. Then God came and turned the light on and made boys and girls and they were *all* special," said one four-year-old happily.

According to Ana-Maria Rizzuto, a Freudian psychoanalyst and the author of *The Birth of the Living God*, at this time an interesting development stems from the child's discarding of the favorite teddy bear or doll known as a transitional object ("cuddly"), which symbolized Mommy and Daddy's love and care and occupied an emotional "space" between parent and child. Now the awareness of God takes form in that same space, only this time without a visible object. At this time—when the child is also grappling with the idea of her parents' mortality— her image of God becomes an idealized version of her mother and father.

Through language, the preschooler is also learning to sort out and express her own emotions. Now vivid religious images, symbols, and stories strike a strong chord in her heart. There is an unpredictability to her responses, because she is still in the process of constructing her worldview without logical tools, and parents often have to "wing it," relying mostly on nonverbal reassurance to convey their love even as she responds to these symbols. Once, on a visit to an art museum with my three-year-old, I tried to hurry her past a room filled with paintings of the crucifixion. But a portrait of Christ wearing a crown of thorns caught her eye, and she refused to budge. "Why is Jesus bleeding?" she asked. Her Sunday school curriculum had, quite appropriately, always shown him smiling.

"Those branches he's wearing on his head have prickers on them," I said quickly, stooping to pick her up and carry her out of the room.

But she squirmed out of my arms. "Why is he wearing branches?"

"Well, some people were making fun of him because he said he was a king, and they wanted to put a pretend crown on him," I replied. "Now why don't we go into the next room where they have lots of nice pictures of babies and flowers?" I kissed her cheek.

"Is he sad?" she persisted.

"Yes, the person who painted the picture is showing us that Jesus felt very sad."

"Did he die?"

"Yes," I said, "he died on the cross."

"Well, anyway," she reflected, her voice trembling, "in the spring, his daddy will make him alive again!"

Logical concepts such as the difference between a picture and a living person, or between events past and present, were beyond my daughter at this point. There was no sense in trying to "correct" her. And after all, in three-year-old terms—intermingling reality and fantasy, and expressing her own feelings about pain and death—she had been touched by the themes of suffering and rebirth which for Christians are the Easter message of hope.

Unfortunately, the young child's immediate apprehension of images does not always inspire hope. She is highly susceptible to frightening ones. And because at this age she is in the process of developing a sense of right and wrong and an awareness of parental authority, she soaks up images of a wrathful God like a small sponge. For this reason, although our religious traditions do include stories of God's anger toward humanity, it is wise to postpone these until the time when our child is emotionally and intellectually prepared for them. The psychologist Dr. Bruno Bettelheim observes in *The Uses of Enchantment*,

. . . from four until puberty, what the child needs most is to be presented with symbolic images which reassure him. . . . [R]eassurance about a happy outcome has to come first. . . . As the story of Cain and Abel shows, there is no sympathy in the Bible for the agonies of sibling rivalry—only a warning that acting upon it has devastating consequences. But what a child needs most, when beset by jealousy of his sibling, is the permission to feel that what he experiences is justified by the situation he is in.

During these early years, our child is continually seeking answers to life's most basic questions in highly personal terms: "What should I become? Is there hope for me, even though I am small and sometimes even bad? Are my parents and other people in charge—including God—loving and fair?" She will find nurture in stories that offer reassurance of love, hope, and the wonder of creation. This does not mean that we need to ignore the existence of evil, or avoid struggle; our children recognize these as part of life, whether they are personified by fairy-tale villains or Philistines. But this is a sensitive age, when the child is open to the images she is exposed to, and for this reason we need to be especially careful about the kind of Sunday school lessons she is hearing. Stories of lasting love and heroes who emerge victorious—David and Goliath, Daniel in the lions' den, Ruth, the good Samaritan—are appropriate for preschoolers. There is no need to tell a young child about Cain and Abel, or the fall of Sodom and Gomorrah, or the crucifixion, simply because they happen to be included in our illustrated children's Bible.

"When I bought a version of the story of Noah, I picked one that doesn't make a big deal about God getting angry at the people," said one mother of two boys. "We talk a lot about the rainbow."

       "But isn't everything here green?" asked Dorothy.

    "No more than in any other city," replied Oz; "but when you wear green spectacles, why of course everything you see looks green to you. . . . But my people have worn green glasses on their eyes so long that most of them think it really is an Emerald City, and it certainly is a beautiful place, abounding in jewels and precious metals, and every good thing that is needed to make one happy."

The school years. "I don't think there really is a God who can see what I'm doing or knows what I'm thinking," said one six-year-old hesitantly. It was a remark typical of the transition to middle childhood, a time when children are struggling to sort out what is real from what is imagined.

The summer before Georgie entered the first grade, he overheard his mother gossiping on the telephone about an acquaintance who, in her words, was "such a fundamentalist that she actually *believes* the story of Adam and Eve." That September, Georgie was enrolled in Sunday school.

He emerged from the first class looking discouraged, and even a bit insulted. "How was it?" his mother inquired.

"Stupid," said Georgie. "The teacher is dumb."

"Dumb?" repeated his mother. "Why do you say that?" As she spoke, she glanced down at the instruction booklet Georgie had received in class. The first lesson, she noticed, had been a simplified version of the creation stories in Genesis.

Georgie sighed. "The teacher thinks Adam and Eve were really alive!" he said disgustedly. "*We* don't believe in Adam and Eve do we, Mom? I heard you say they weren't real!"

Georgie, true to his age, had become a "realist." In using this term, it is important to keep in mind that the realism of a seven-year-old is considerably different from that of an adult. Up until the age of seven or eight, the child casually juxtaposes fantasy and reality, no matter how contradictory they may seem to us. To use Fowler's terms, the young child makes "intuitive" observations of the world, by "projecting" her own self-centered inner universe onto everything she sees. "The child often sees only what he already knows," observed Jean Piaget, who pioneered in the study of children's thought processes. "He projects the whole of his verbal thought into things. He sees mountains as built by men, rivers as dug out with spades, the sun and moon as following us on our walks."

But now, by the time the child reaches the first or second grade, she is capable of more objective observation of the world around her, and she seeks consistency. "Reality" is now associated with that which can be seen or touched. She is capable of considerable logical reasoning about an object or situation, and is eager to "understand" it by learning endless details about its size, origins, and use. Piaget called this stage of reasoning "concrete operations." This newly acquired ability to reason does not apply to abstract concepts. In the mind of the concrete operational child, all that which is known only verbally—stories, unseen beings, and ideas, for example—is relegated to the realm of the "*not* real." Spiritually speaking, she is like the person from Missouri; "show me," she demands, which helps explain the persistent inquiries about the mechanics of reaching the afterlife and the insistence on physical descriptions of God. "Is there a real tooth fairy?" one six-year-old asked his mother in a doubtful tone.

"I think there might be," she replied.

"Just like there might be a God?" he shot back.

One mother found her six-year-old, who had been taught that God is "everywhere," frantically searching for God in the closet in his room. A seven-year-old girl wondered whether God was inside her stomach. Another child, told that God sends sunlight to make the plants grow, exclaimed, "Yes, Jesus rides across the sky on a sunbeam!"

One little boy was puzzled after attending a children's service led by a guitar-playing minister who led the group in "He's Got the Whole World in His Hands."

"*Who's* got the whole world in his hands?" he inquired.

Over lunch that day, he clapped his hands suddenly. "I figured it out!" he exclaimed.

"What?" asked his puzzled parents.

"I figured out who's got the whole world in his hands!"

"Who?"

The small voice was triumphant: *"Atlas!"*

Often we wish our children could understand certain subtleties. Georgie's mother, for example, tried to explain to him that although certain stories may not be "really true, they tell us something true. Even if Adam and Eve didn't really live, the story tells us that God made the first people and he knew they were good." Not surprisingly, Georgie simply stared at her blankly. He will not be capable of such abstract thinking until he is close to puberty.

In talking with my own children about God, I have always tried to convey a sense of God's presence in people and in nature, rather than on some distant heavenly throne. One summer's day, after I had picked up my son from day camp, we were having lunch at the kitchen table when he burst out indignantly, "The boys at camp say God is invisible!"

"Well, he is——" I began, then stopped myself. "You don't think he is?"

"Of course not," he replied, almost scornfully. "*Anyone* can see God—the sun, the leaves, the people we love. *You* know!"

There is no child in our society, according to Dr. Rizzuto, who does not, by the age of six, construct some representation of God. It may not be a positive image to which she feels attached or inclined to pray—and may be a conglomeration of superheroes drawn from the media—but it is that of a being with a point of view distinct from her own.

Because she thinks in concrete terms, the school-age child is unlikely to accept an amorphous image of God. The image of an old man with a beard, or the person of Jesus for a child growing up in the Christian tradition, is likely to appeal to the young school-age child. Although parents are often uncomfortable with such an anthropomorphic image, the child who is actively prevented from conceptualizing God in this way now will find it difficult to relate to God as a being rather than an inanimate object. If God is not understood as a person at this age, one writer suggested, God can be little more than tapioca.

Likewise, the school-age child delights in traditional religious symbols, action-packed Bible stories, and holiday rituals that involve the people and community of which she is so happy to be a part. For the child of this age, the religious rituals and symbols she learns at home and in her own faith community embody "reality" about God and spirituality. At this stage, according to Fowler, she is in the "mythic-literal" stage of faith, when she is interested in stories and understands everything concretely. And herein lies the paradox of the spiritual nurture of the elementary-school child. Unlike her squirming and often-bewildered younger sibling, she is ready and often willing to learn about that which we think of as "religion." She is delighted to wear her Sunday school pin, to ask the Four Questions at the seder, to be Mary in the Christmas pageant. No matter how hard we try to offer "enlightened" explanations, she eagerly embraces the rituals at face value.

In their determination to cling to the "real" truth, children of this age can be embarrassingly ruthless in their dismissal of other people's religious beliefs.

Elizabeth, a former Roman Catholic whose Jewish husband is raising their three boys in his family's tradition, recalled an embarrassing moment in the first-grade car pool. As her son Bart buckled up in the backseat, he turned to the little girl beside him, whose family attends a Protestant church. "You know, Jesus wasn't God," he said matter-of-factly, "and he's dead now."

Later on that day Elizabeth told him, "It's not really a good idea to say that kind of thing to people of other religions. They have their beliefs, and we have our own."

"Well, she's only going to find out the hard way after she dies!" Bart retorted. "She'll get to heaven, and God will say, 'Jews, you were *right*.'"

We all know adults, of various religious backgrounds, whose thinking is equally narrow-minded, of course. And some religious educators have suggested that when our teaching panders to the elementary-school child's concrete thinking, we are encouraging her to become trapped in the *forms* of religion and actually crippling her spiritually. The British religious educator Ronald Goldman has compared rote religious instruction at this age to teaching a child the multiplication tables before she has had the opportunity to acquire a concept of number by playing with blocks. "There is strong and disturbing evidence to indicate that a great deal of religious teaching merely reinforces crude, sub-religious thought . . ." Goldman warns. "Their imprisonment within concrete concepts and their frequent literalisms make it difficult for them to step forward into a more spiritual understanding of religious truth."

Does this mean that we ought to *avoid* traditional religious teaching at this age? Not at all. There are two primary ways we can help the child's thinking lead to, rather than hamper, spiritual growth. First, we can present religious concepts in terms of her own concrete everyday *experiences*. If she asks about God's creation of the world, for example, we need not stammer endless explanations about the way the Genesis accounts relate to evolution. Instead, we can ask our child to remember a time when *she* made something very special, such as an art project. How did she feel about it? Does she keep it in a safe place and take care of it? Why? Then we can encourage her to imagine how God feels about the world God made.

Second, we can keep in mind that our child's spiritual growth does not depend solely on the *content* of religious instruction. Rather than spoon-feeding her information—on saints' lives, biblical battles, and church rules—which she is bound to swallow whole and never really digest, we can help her explore her spiritual connections firsthand. Now that she is interested in the ideas and perspectives of others, she can grow through participation in a faith community, helping out at mealtimes, saying grace, participating in food drives.

As a child reaches adolescence and her thinking becomes increasingly abstract, the concrete images she has acquired are likely to be called into question. She will move into the stage

Fowler terms "synthetic-conventional," when her view of the world will be based on the expectations and judgments she hears in school, and work, and among peers. Becoming aware of others' expectations and internalizing them, she will accept *symbols* of her peer group—whether these are a particular liturgy, if she is part of a faith community, or a style of dress and speech borrowed from a favorite rock group—as sacred in themselves.

If she is not to cling to the mere trappings of religion (or music television) but discover a path to growth, she will need to come to her *own* faith through critical reflection. She will struggle with doubt and inevitably some of life's pain before she comes to a mature acceptance—or rejection—of the tenets of her childhood religious faith. She will notice the very real gap between biblical values and her own faith community.

At this time what she will need most of all are loving adults and a peer group with whom she can share her questions and feelings. The *ideas* that shape her spirituality—love, justice, forgiveness, hope—will be tested against her *experience* in family and community.

* * *

Of course each one of them expected to see the Wizard in the shape he had taken before . . .

Not surprisingly, spiritual nurture is not "dispensed" through a series of specific hands-on activities, or through a set of developmentally appropriate answers to Important Questions. It is part of all the humble, unpredictable moments of life with children. We water the houseplants together. A pet turtle dies. In the midst of a traffic jam, a small voice from the backseat announces, "God is the whole sky." In this section you will find approaches to spiritual nurture at each stage of a child's development.

One caveat: Although the developmental signposts in this chapter help us make sense of our child's spirituality, it is important to know that they are not the whole story. As we listen with open hearts to our child's thoughts and concerns, and as we continue to explore our own spirituality, we make a surprising discovery. Together we are learning and growing, not by formula but by inspiration.

Infants: welcome to the world. Perhaps there is no other time when spiritual nurture is so obviously embodied in flesh and blood than during a child's first two years of life. It happens in many ways that sensitive parents have always known. As the baby's *trust* develops through everyday care, God's love is a warm nipple. During the early months, we offer spiritual nurture in the exhausting, endless caring that fills our days. Together we enjoy skin-to-skin contact as we give her a bath, carry her in a front pack, hold her during a feeding. She cries, and we begin to understand whether she needs food or sleep or a dry diaper or a change of scenery. For the baby, gripping our extended forefingers while sitting up in our lap is an experience of trust. With the smiles and admiring glances that convey our love and affirmation, we show her the eyes that recognize and the face that blesses.

Of course, she also enjoys playing in an infant seat, or lying on the floor on a blanket, where she can see our comings and goings. In this way she comes to know that we can go out of sight and return. A teddy bear, a small doll, or even something that belongs to Mom (a soft scarf or a nightgown) can help her feel the comfort of a parent's presence even when we are not in the room. And, knowing that her sense of trust grows out of continuity and dependence, we protect it by seeking reliable, stable care givers.

We can nurture a child's emerging sense of *self* in many different ways. We can recognize that each baby has a different temperament. Some love to be held and cuddled, while others are so sensitive to touch that it makes them irritable. Some eat quickly, all gasps and gulps; others are constantly dozing off.

Propped up in the infant seat—watching the family eat dinner, or seeing Mom and Dad tidy up the living room—she discovers that the world is a fascinating place, full of moving shapes and colors. Crumpling a piece of aluminum foil on the high-chair tray is a moment of wonder. We can offer rattles of various shapes and sizes, musical toys, soft balls, wooden spoons, and other safe household objects of different shapes and patterns. We can hang toys and rattles from the high-chair or stroller handle so that she can bat at them. As she begins to creep, we can child-proof our home and offer her plenty of opportunities to explore. All this we do not to transform her into a prodigy, but to enable her to discover her own active connections with the world around her.

From the start we can respond to her natural attempts at *communicating*. She is eager for eye contact after a nap, and we realize it is a good time to bring out her favorite rattle and exchange giggles.

She gurgles and babbles, and we gurgle and babble back. She smiles at the sight of a butterfly, and we supply her with the words to express her excitement: "What a pretty butterfly! Pretty yellow!" We respond to her gestures. "Juice?" we ask as she points to the refrigerator. "You want juice?" We cannot always give her what she asks for, of course, but we can acknowledge her request: "A cookie? You want a *cookie*? You must be teasing me! We don't have cookies for *breakfast*, do we? How about a piece of toast?"

We also show respect for her as a separate person by understanding that sometimes she does not wish to communicate. We notice that she looks drowsy, avoids our gaze, turns away her head, or even arches her body away, and we know that she is not interested in play. Reading our baby's cues in this way is not always easy. For so many months, she was a beloved extension of ourselves who happily slept and squirmed in the womb; suddenly we are aware that she is a small person who is shy or outgoing, placid or demanding, and her style may be startlingly different from our own.

By eight months or so, we begin to share everyday *rituals* and to appreciate the comfort she takes in them. In the morning as she spoons rice cereal all over her face, we carry on a "conversation" together. By the time she is nine or ten months we "read" stories like *Pat the Bunny* over and over and let her enjoy turning the pages and touching the familiar textures. We can also include her in adult rituals; they will have no symbolic meaning for her now, of course, but are lovely early images of special family times. She can watch the candle flames during the lighting of the menorah; she enjoys shaking jingle bells while we sing Christmas carols. (My son's very first word came at Christmastime, as he pointed to the light-bedecked Douglas fir in our living room and exclaimed, "Tee!")

Like newborn babes, long for the pure spiritual milk . . .
—1 Peter 2:2

The toddler. The child's own sense of self emerges with force during the second year. Now she walks independently and speaks in two- and three-word sentences. This is a time when she is frequently testing *limits*. Her early sentences are more than likely to be challenges. But she is not so much trying to rebel as to understand and experiment with rules about everything from using the toilet to sleeping to touching electrical sockets. "No!" is one of her very favorite words. We can encourage her to continue to explore *safely* by providing a child-proof environment and offering opportunities to make messes in ways that minimize the mess—in a sandbox, or at the kitchen sink at convenient times.

There are times when we do need to reprimand her, of course. In scolding her out of a desire to protect her and help her grow, we are offering a valuable lesson in the way love and discipline come together. As we discussed in chapter 4, we are assuring her that, even with all her flaws, she is deeply loved.

Another challenge for the parents of a toddler is the strange ideas she gets that leave her—and us—feeling terribly frustrated. A broken cookie is not edible. A shirt with a spot of spaghetti sauce on it must be changed. A sandwich cut the "wrong" way—diagonally instead of horizontally—is not an acceptable lunch. And when the small block tower she is building topples, she dissolves in tears.

No parent finds it easy to deal with a toddler's unreasonable expectations. Yet we can avoid frustration by understanding them as signs that she has begun to realize that there are "rules" and "standards" of behavior in the adult world. She is not sure what those "rules" are yet, and any departure from what she is used to is likely to fill her with alarm. She is not *trying* to be difficult. She needs our quiet reassurance that she is loved and valued as we help her arrive at more realistic standards. Rather than denying or discounting her feelings ("It's only a block tower!"), we can supply words to help her express her frustration ("Boom! It fell down! And after all that work"), and then offer reassurance and support ("I wonder how long it would take us to build it up again? Let's start with the bottom floor"). Not exactly the kind of nurture we might think of as "spiritual." And yet in the process we communicate the empathy and love and hope of our sacred bonds as parent and child.

Ages three to five: hands-on activities, fantasy play. The preschool child enjoys opportunities to integrate stories with creative activities and pretend play. She likes to help out with holiday projects—making potato pancakes, dyeing Easter eggs. If she says grace at meals, she will give thanks for everything from a new bike to the ice-cream pops in the freezer. When a pet dies, she will appreciate the opportunity to participate in a funeral. To pretend to be Jesus or Judah Maccabee is not too different from playing Batman or Superman. To be Mary is to cradle a doll in her arms and gently rock it to sleep. By providing dress-up clothes (leftover lengths of fabric make wonderful Middle Eastern garb), pretend-play materials (small figures, a Noah's ark set, an unbreakable manger scene), and art materials, we offer her opportunities to incorporate stories and traditions into her playtime. She is exploring her own feelings and experiences, coming to know herself and the world around her. As she shares her impressions with us—no matter how outlandish they seem—there is no need to correct her. She grows as we listen attentively and continue to offer more stories and materials to encourage her explorations.

Because she is still spontaneous and full of wonder, she delights in encounters with the natural world. The first daffodil of springtime is cause for celebration. Every caterpillar is about to turn into a butterfly. "Whee!" she cries as she rolls down a grass-covered slope for the eighth time.

She is interested in Bible stories when she can actively

connect them with her own inner drama—her awakening experiences of loss and fear, her sense that she is a small person in a big, sometimes scary world—and with her frequent musings about the nature of things. Why do people die? Why do some children misbehave? Why do Mommy and Daddy scold me? For this reason, we need only tell the stories in simple language, and allow her to interpret them as she wishes.

As we have already seen, young children tend to interpret everything so literally that many religious educators and theologians have suggested that it is wiser to postpone Bible reading until children are old enough to think critically. "It is true, of course, that children think in graphic, dramatic images," wrote Karl Rahner (in *The Practice of Faith*). "But this is no proof that, for example, the Bible stories about the Garden of Paradise, the fall of Adam, and so on are appropriate material as children's stories, or that they do not do more harm than good to the faith later on, having been understood childishly in the first place."

On the other hand, many parents and educators feel that a lifelong familiarity with at least *some* of the stories in the Bible is a precious gift. A child who hears the story of David and Goliath gains an understanding of heroism and God's empowerment of the underdog to be held in his heart long after the memory of television superheroes has faded. He is discovering that these stories, and the traditions they represent, speak to his deepest self.

"Knowledge of Scriptures has never cramped a child's spirit," writes the Quaker sociologist and pacifist Elise Boulding bluntly; "the cramping comes only through the lifeless rendition of Scriptures by uncomprehending adults." If, in our heart of hearts, we think of biblical characters as a group of edifying personages our child probably ought to know "for his own good," he is bound to get the message—and resist.

...As They Grow

A mother and small boy are standing in the children's section of a bookstore. "What books do they have?" asks the child, who looks about four years old.

"Well, they have the adventures of the explorers . . ."

"I want *that* one!" he interrupts.

". . . the Vikings . . ."

"I want *that* one, too!"

". . . and the lives of heroes of the Bible."

Pause. "I don't think I'd be very interested in *that*."

For the most part, the "heroes" of the Bible are an unremarkable lot. They are teachers, mothers, fathers, and children who go on trips together, grow gardens, care for their families, work hard for a living. The stories about them are accounts of how God acts in the lives of ordinary people. As we share them with our children, we need not attempt to draw any earth-shattering conclusions. We need only be quietly open to noticing the ways in which the stories reflect our own daily experiences.

For this reason, the stories we can share most effectively are the ones that mean something in our own lives. We need not start with Adam and Eve and plow straight through an illustrated children's Bible. Instead, we can choose *one* story we may have enjoyed as a child, reread it ahead of time, and then read it aloud—or, better still—*tell* it in our own words. (Suffering through stilted, archaic language is certainly not required; after all, these stories were passed down orally for generations before they were ever written down.) Speak slowly, and expect younger children, in particular, to interrupt with plenty of questions. And there's no need to offer a "moral"; just share the story. The myths speaks to the child where she is. After the story, try to spend a few unhurried moments with your child as she replays it in her mind (usually out loud). If she is not pressured to do so, she may enjoy telling *you* the story later on. Providing related materials—for pretend-play (with character dolls, for example, or a molded plastic Noah's Ark set) or to help narrow the culture gap (musical instruments, bread, and so on)—can be helpful. (*For more information on telling Bible stories, see the appendix.*)

Early school age: sharing the stories. The child is full of energy now. She is learning to think logically about concrete facts and experiences. She is still egocentric, but she is increasingly aware of the rules and demands of friendship and acceptable behavior. Morality is embodied not only in parents but in teachers, too, and God is likely to be imagined as a human figure—a rather authoritarian one, at that.

When one seven-year-old overheard his three-year-old sister comment happily, "We belong to God," he gave her an angry look.

"*I* don't!" he retorted.

"Yes, you do," she said. "We all do."

"Well," replied the seven-year-old gloomily, "I don't *want* to."

Not only does the child of this age often have a rather daunting image of God, but she is likely to see the characters in the Bible as part of a far-off, imaginary world where people wear long outfits, tend sheep, and talk to angels. She is not uninterested in fantasy as a part of *play*, but *real* life is beginning to look like "just the facts, ma'am," which seems to leave aside spiritual matters. For this reason, she will be most responsive to spiritual nurture—at home, and in religious school or camp—that satisfies her hunger to learn about the "real world."

By reading about and discussing the lives of heroes past and present—from Washington to Lincoln to Mother Teresa to the volunteers at the local soup kitchen—we help her understand that God is at work not only in distant deserts, but also in the lives of real people. She is ready to hear not only victory stories, but also those that depict life as hard at times. She is receptive to the idea that the journey is smoother when we stick together.

Through walks, books, and museum visits, we can help her explore natural phenomena—seeds, insects, sand, space—conveying the "facts" with reverence and wonder. In low-key ways, we help her understand that spirituality is not a part of our lives in opposition to science or history, but that which gives them meaning and purpose.

For now, despite our best efforts, her formal religious concepts are likely to remain surprisingly literal. We need not "plant weeds," in rabbi and author Harold Kushner's phrase, by reinforcing her overly concrete ideas about God. There is no point in encouraging her to pray for new toys, or in suggesting that God will punish her when she misbehaves. As she grows toward adolescence, she will begin to look beyond her literal ideas, to question and doubt.

Having avoided depicting God as Santa Claus, or religion as the emotional equivalent of wearing our "Sunday best," we will have laid the groundwork for deeper probing. At this age, the child is delighted to find out what "we" believe, and will enjoy learning the stories and traditions of her own religious denomination. But at the same time, if her religious education is to be something more than a method of indoctrinating her into a particular institutional church, she needs to be encouraged to think critically and to recognize the challenges presented by her tradition. She needs to be able to question the ideas presented in Sunday school, if only to be allowed to complain that it's boring.

She needs to be encouraged to ask "Why?" and to use her imagination. Making a list of ideas for a safer environment in honor of Earth Day, or doing a poster about world peace, or singing songs about the human family will help expand her horizons. As she gives thanks at dinner for her own meal, we can show her photographs of children in other countries who eat different food. When she gets excited about Easter or Christmas, we can teach her about Passover or Chanukah; because she enjoys understanding things from another's perspective, she is fascinated with hearing how other people celebrate holidays.

She needs to be reminded that there is always more to discover. For now, we can use her concreteness to *expand* her understanding of religious concepts by drawing on her own experience.

"It's hard to believe God could be a father and a son at the same time," said one eight-year-old after hearing the Christian doctrine of the Trinity.

"It *is* hard," I said. What meaning could such a difficult theological concept have for a second-grader? I asked myself. "What do fathers do?" I ventured.

"They take care of us and love us," she said.

I agreed, and added that without our fathers, we wouldn't have been born.

"That's right, our fathers *make* us," she said.

"Okay, so that's what fathers do." So far so good. "Now what about children?" I asked. "How does a baby make you feel?"

"Like hugging and loving it," she said.

"Yes . . . Well, then what would it mean if God is a father and a son?"

"That he made us, and takes care of us, and we love him," she answered.

It wasn't exactly the way *I* remember learning the Trinity as a kid. Conversations don't always wrap up quite so neatly, of course, and we hadn't explored any feminine images of God, but this seemed to mark a promising beginning.

As the school-age child continues to ask challenging questions, she will struggle—with her own experience and with more complex ideas—toward a more mature spirituality.

The deities of some are in water, those of the more advanced are in the heavens, those of the children (in religion) are in images of wood and stone, but the sage finds God in his deeper self.

—Upanishads

By adolescence, the child will enter what Fowler calls the "synthetic-conventional" stage of faith and base her worldview on what she knows from personal relationships. Now she understands beliefs and values as being part of what "kind of person" one is, and mirrors the spirituality she sees around her. The danger of this stage is twofold: Her "spirituality" may be a reflection of values (those of the drug culture, consumerism, satanic cults, etc.) that will ultimately fail to sustain her. Or, if she is part of an institutional church, at some point (usually after a personal disappointment) she may decide that she is no longer "part of the group" and will discard her spirituality altogether.

Most people remain at this conventional stage, according to Fowler, for a lifetime; we affiliate with a particular religion or group because that's what "people like us" are supposed to do. If we are to help our child grow beyond conventional thinking and *own* her spirituality, we need to offer her the critical tools to begin to do so. We will need to be sure, in a youth group setting or among peers, that she has access to adults who are willing really to listen as she shares her own experiences and reflects on how she has come to them. In a nonjudgmental way, they can help her connect her own life with the stories and vision of generations past. Only then will her spirituality continue to deepen.

7. Play Is a Child's Prayer

*. . . she held back the swinging curtain of
ivy and pushed back the door which opened
slowly—slowly.*

*Then she slipped through it, and shut it
behind her, and stood with her back against it,
looking about her and breathing quite fast
with her excitement, and wonder, and
delight.*

She was standing inside the secret garden.

——*THE SECRET GARDEN*,
FRANCES HODGSON BURNETT

When we first meet Mary Lennox in *The Secret Garden*, she is a
dour, passive nine-year-old who hardly seems at all like a child.
Brought up by servants in colonial India until her parents died
of cholera, she is used to being entertained and waited on, to
simply "stand and allow herself to be dressed like a doll." Now
that she has come to live on her uncle's estate in Yorkshire,
her senses and imagination are awakening as she learns to do
and discover things for herself.

The turning point in Mary's sad, young life comes on the

day when she receives a special gift: a skipping-rope. On that unforgettable day, as she skips merrily up and down the walk around the orchard, feeling the sun shining and a breeze blowing—really *playing* for the first time in her life—Mary discovers the secret garden that is to become for her a source of continuing joy and renewal.

Play is a child's prayer. For a child, to play is to pray. True child's play opens the door to a life of true prayer, just as surely as Mary's skipping down the path leads her to the garden door. Prayer as play may sound like a revolutionary idea, but it has long been recognized as such in various religious traditions. To set aside "productive" work and leave room in the week for "useless" activities that seem to open us up to the sacred: this has always been the gift of the Sabbath.

The child who picks up a stick and imagines it as a sword, or as a conductor's baton, or as a magic wand, is blessed with a fresh perception of the world, a glimpse beyond the boundaries of visible reality. "The wise man knows that imagination is not only a means of pleasing himself and beguiling tedious hours with romances and fairy tales," wrote George Bernard Shaw, "but also a means of foreseeing and being prepared for realities as yet unexperienced, and of testing the possibility and desirability of serious Utopias."

The child who runs and jumps on a playground knows unbridled joy, like David, who danced before the Lord with all his might when the ark was brought to Jerusalem.

And the child who loses herself in the world of play knows what it is to live in the present moment.

Simplicity, insight, and presence: these are the deepest rewards of adult contemplative prayer described by spiritual masters through the centuries. They are the child's gifts in play.

. . . Play Is a Child's Prayer

They always called it Magic and indeed it seemed like it in the months that followed—the wonderful months—the radiant months—the amazing ones. Oh! the things which happened in that garden! If you have never had a garden, you cannot understand, and if you have had a garden you will know that it would take a whole book to describe all that came to pass here.

Do you remember how Mary Lennox and her two friends Dickon and Colin sense the presence of a mysterious, life-giving source in the secret garden they tend? "*Something* is there— *something*!" says Colin, the ten-year-old invalid. What is there is a nurturing presence the children come to call "the Magic." Their time spent with the Magic in the secret garden—digging, planting, reaping, and simply *being*—is prayer. The children do not actually *say* a prayer, in any formal sense, until the very end of the book, when they want to shout out that they are "thankful to the Magic," as Colin puts it. But that spoken prayer is a response to their work and play in the garden, and to their wonder at the roses and iris and delphiniums that are the garden's gifts.

For this reason, to nurture a child's prayer has very little to do with teaching him to kneel beside his bed with hands sweetly folded, in the manner of a Norman Rockwell illustration. Prayer is not something a child learns in religious school. All children pray, until we teach them not to. To pray, the rabbi Abraham Joshua Heschel wrote, is to "nurse the song in the recesses of the soul." The child—the spontaneous creature who hails the first snowfall with whoops of joy, who speaks with delightful candor, and who exults in the simple pleasure of stomping in a rain puddle—has the song not in his soul's recesses, but on his lips.

Religion, where spiritual nurture is concerned, is a seed catalog. Religion—doctrine, ritual, and history—offers the tools we need, the instructions for planting, and the description of the garden, which is the abundant life of the spirit. But religion alone is lifeless. Prayer is the seed that grows into the garden.

Prayer is not a seed most of us are used to cultivating, of course. We tend to think of it, if we think of it at all, as wishful thinking. It is an attempt to communicate on a cosmic walkie-talkie that seems to have a great deal of static on the line. "When I was a child I had a mental image of someone I could call God—a man with a white beard sitting on a cloud," said one mother. "Once I discarded that image, prayer didn't seem to make much sense anymore. How do you talk to someone, or something, when you don't know who or what it is?"

Prayer in its most profound sense does not refer to *saying* something. It is not a recitation of pious phrases. Many of us begin to find our way to prayer by understanding it as *listening* to God, as a setting aside of the day's busyness to hear the eternal voice in silence.

Yet prayer goes deeper, even, than listening. True prayer, as spiritual masters have written for millennia, is an *attitude* cultivated throughout the day. "Prayer is the effort to live in the spirit of the whole," wrote Coleridge. It is the planting of the religion's catalog in the home soil of the heart, the humble attending to everyday miracle. Moments when we consciously do what we call "praying" are really opportunities to deepen the attitude which is true prayer. "The moment of prayer is for me . . . ," C. S. Lewis wrote, "the awareness, the reawakened awareness, that this 'real world' and 'real self' are very far from being rock-bottom realities." To pray is to recognize consciously the presence of the sacred within and beyond the self. It is to willingly open the heart to life at its deepest source. It is to know how to live from moment to moment with the trust and wonder of a child.

In this chapter we shall explore the various ways we can nurture true prayer in our children through play, silence, and the spoken word.

> *Mary glanced about her. There was nothing to do. When Mrs. Medlock had prepared the nursery she had not thought of amusement.*

Play as prayer is not an activity we need to plan for our children. In fact, we *cannot* plan it, because it is play's unguarded spontaneity that makes it a valuable part of spiritual nurture. Play as prayer is the opposite of the "play with a purpose" our generation of parents has heard so much about. We need to reassure ourselves that, like Mary Lennox, our children can benefit from having "nothing to do."

This is no small challenge in our busy lives as families, where intervals between structured, educational programs and activities are brief, and we may be so worried that our children are "bored" that we fill their free time with television and video games. "Sometimes I worry about the amount of time Davey spends with Nintendo," said one mother of a four-year-old. "I think it would probably be a lot better for him to be zooming trucks around the playroom. But he does seem to *learn* a lot from video games—eye-hand coordination and all that."

We can pore over endless studies about the *cognitive* skills to be learned through television and video games, workbooks, and highly structured educational toys. But as we seek to offer spiritual nurture, these studies do not address the questions that are truly central. How can children come to know themselves when their playtime is consumed in passive entertainment? How can they hold on to their natural spontaneity and wonder when instead we teach them to be "fulfilled" at the push of a button?

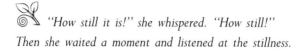

"How still it is!" she whispered. "How still!"
Then she waited a moment and listened at the stillness.

Silence is not something we tend to associate with our children. The moment we begin to suspect they are "too quiet," don't we all rush off to find out what mischief they're up to?

We may even assume that silence is a waste of time for children, who have so much to learn. "If we're waiting in the doctor's office or in line somewhere, I try to get my daughter thinking, rather than just sitting there letting our minds do nothing," one mother of a five-year-old girl told me. "So I drill her any time we have the chance—letters, numbers, parts of the body."

Far from being a waste of time, the quiet, unproductive moments in our children's lives can be profoundly meaningful and sustaining. Silence should not be forced on a child. Yet it can be presented as an opportunity for us to set aside the day's cares so that we can be attentive to and aware of the deeper truths that speak within our hearts, to "listen at the stillness." In his *Memoirs of a Quaker Boyhood*, Rufus Jones recalled his own early appreciation of silence during Quaker meetings:

. . . Play Is a Child's Prayer

It might be supposed that a little boy, keyed to action and charged with animal spirits, on a hard bench, with feet unsupported, would have hated this silence and would have longed for a chance to hit the boy in the next seat over the head. But that was not the case. Sooner or later the boy would get hit no doubt when the proper time came for it. But the silence came over us as a kind of spell. It had a life of its own. There was something "numinous" about it, which means, in simpler non-Latin words, a sense of divine presence, which even a boy could feel.

Jones points out that he was never offered a formal explanation or doctrine of the purpose of silence. He was simply allowed to *encounter* it. "We found ourselves in the midst of a unique laboratory experiment which *worked*," he recalls. As he grew to adulthood, his early encounters with silence stayed with him. "That experiment with silence in the far-off period of my youth, sitting in the hush with the moveless group, concentrated on the expectation of divine presence, did something to me and for me which has remained an unlost possession."

The Italian educator Maria Montessori observed that children are well aware of the richness and fullness of silence. In her Children's Houses in the slums of Rome, she introduced what she called "the silence lesson." As she began to write the word *silence* on the blackboard, she noted, the whole class would stop working and become perfectly still before she had even finished writing. Children as young as three "took pleasure" in silence, Montessori found, "like ships safe in a tranquil harbour."

Without any instruction at all, even the youngest child can discover the presence that speaks in the absence of noise. Once I confessed to a group of first-graders that as a child I thought

God's voice was supposed to boom out from underneath the altar in church. "Well, it doesn't," said one little girl in a condescending tone. "God talks in our *hearts.*"

I asked a group of six-year-olds whether they had ever felt God was with them, and one child, whom I'll call Nina, looked into my eyes for a moment and then said simply, "When I was sick."

"When you were sick?" I replied. "What happened?"

"I had a high fever and I felt God," she answered quietly. "I felt God."

I knew that Nina had been hospitalized at the age of four with a high fever. During those days of solitude, had she really known a spiritual encounter, or could she now be repeating words of comfort her parents had shared with her then? Later on, when I asked her mother, she told me no one had told Nina anything of the kind, and I was not surprised. Nina had spoken with a calm assurance and wisdom far beyond her years. She had been drawn to the heart of silence.

Silence does not often yield such extraordinary gifts. But even seemingly ordinary periods of silence can remain with a child in years to come, a reminder of the value of setting aside daily preoccupations in the face of silence.

"I feel—I feel as if I want to shout out something—something thankful, joyful!"

We yearn to offer our children spiritual nurture, but we probably feel less then enthusiastic about the prospect of praying aloud with them. How can we teach our children to pray aloud when we ourselves are not accustomed to praying, and when we are not at all convinced our prayers are heard? "I've never felt comfortable teaching my kids to pray out loud," said one father I spoke with. "I've never felt any sort of 'presence' I could pray to." For Mark, praying out loud would mean simply reciting empty words, or acting pious. "Outward displays of spirituality—kneeling, reciting prayers—always strike me as hypocritical," he said.

Yet as he described his daily interactions with his children, Mark conveyed a strong desire to share with them his own awareness of the sacred. "I want them to know how much we have to be thankful for, and to realize how wonderful the world really can be," he said. "I try to communicate that in the course of our everyday conversations. The other day David and I were taking a walk, and I told him, 'Look at that sunset, David. Never forget that sunset.'" Mark did not use the word *prayer* in describing these moments with David. His words were not self-consciously pious. Yet spontaneously he had joined his voice to the age-old tradition of offering thanks and praise, of sharing a moment of awareness of the eternal. The name of the Lord is to be praised, wrote the psalmist, "from the rising of the sun to its setting."

Understood in this context, what could be more natural than praying aloud with a child? Think back for a moment to those very first "conversations" that you had with your child as an infant. Do you remember how you pointed out the wonders of the world in *oohs* and *aahs*? "What a pretty flower!" "See the big tree!" "Look at the clouds!" We introduce our children to the world with praise, knowing they will naturally respond to it, if only (in those early days) with wide, alert eyes and an appreciative wriggle.

Sharing prayer aloud can continue to be a natural part of our family lives as our children grow. Rather than worrying about teaching our children the "right" words to use, we need only understand that in praying aloud with them we are giving spoken expression to the prayer in our hearts.

To pray aloud is to discover the gift of attending to everyday miracles *together* with those we love. To pray aloud is to share our concerns for one another, and for the world outside our home, in the community, the country, the world. To pray aloud is to stand together among the weeds and rosebushes, like the children of *The Secret Garden*, and acknowledge that "the Magic" is the source of all life.

Like young Colin, we may make only halting attempts to express this drawing awareness in words: "I feel—I feel as if I want to shout out something—something thankful, joyful!" We need not expect to *teach* our children to pray aloud. But by setting aside times for prayer together, we encourage them to give voice to their own gratitude and concerns. To *share* prayer aloud with our children is to know and to nurture their gifts of trust and wonder, as well as our own. It is to recognize that spiritual nurture draws us closer to the eternal, and to one another as well.

❋   ❋   ❋

 *Their belief in the Magic was an abiding thing.*

Play and prayer. Perhaps the only way to be sure a child has enough unstructured time to play, in today's hectic world, is to *schedule* it just as we would gymnastics and soccer practice. If your child spends most of the day at home, this may mean planning errands to allow your child free time—with the television *off*—after breakfast or lunch. If your toddler or preschooler attends a day-care center or family-care home, be sure he is getting time between organized "activities" (snacks, story time, worksheets) for free play with open-ended materials. School-age children also need time out from activities, television, and homework to unwind and simply *be*.

. . . Play Is a Child's Prayer

Throughout this book you will find suggestions on how a child's spirituality can be fostered through play. Although planning your child's playtime would be a contradiction in terms, you can provide materials that will help involve him in play.

Dress-up clothes encourage him to experiment with different roles and perspectives on the world, to discover in the world of make-believe what it means to slay a dragon, care for a baby, venture out into the wilderness. For the young child this kind of play encourages the development of the inner life, in which his understanding of the world and his own role in it can be tried on a hundred different ways. Children love hats, parents' old clothes, foreign costumes, pretend medals and badges, and play shoes.

Around the age of seven, as a child's thinking becomes more concrete, he may show less interest in pretend play, but continuing to encourage it is important, since it keeps his mind open to ideas and dreams beyond what his newly "logical" mind would teach him. Do you remember how, according to legend, Merlin the magician instructed the young Arthur in the ways of wisdom? He changed the boy into other creatures—a hawk, a fish, a fox—to offer him a view of life from many different perspectives. Puppets, dress-up-clothes, small play figures and dolls provide opportunities for your child to stage her own made-up stories, and to reenact those you read aloud together until they become her own. One four-year-old boy wore a shepherd's cloak made out of a length of cotton fabric and spent many hours playing David to an invisible Goliath. As most parents notice, pretend-play is an opportunity for a child to act out her own conflicts, from rivalry with a brother or sister to sadness at an absent parent; a willingness to acknowledge these is an essential part of adult prayer.

Art materials. Crayons, paints, clay, play dough, modeling wax, and assorted items for collage-making (elbow macaroni, glitter, magazine pictures, bits of fabric and paper—feed the imagination and offer the child opportunity to express emotions.

Equipment for active play. Running, jumping, climbing, dancing: there is exhilaration about a child's usual means of locomotion, and these are an early encounter to the unity of mind, body, and spirit human beings know in prayer. How difficult it is for us to bring our whole bodies to prayer and meditation, instead of just our frantically busy minds! By encouraging our children to know their bodies as God's precious gifts—with access to a climbing frame, rope ladder, bicycle, ball, swing, slide, and other indoor and outdoor toys—we encourage them to keep body and soul together.

Humor. Joke books, funny poems, and silly stories always delight children, and humor has a way of opening our eyes to the world around us, awakening us to the wonder and puzzlement of life. This frolicsome approach to spirituality has a long history in various traditions, from the Eastern Orthodox "holy fool" to the Tibetan Buddhist "crazy wisdom" to Yiddish humor. What could be a more appropriate form of spiritual nurture for kids? Even a one-year-old laughs when Daddy wears a diaper on his head, and a six-year-old's passion for joke-telling rivals that of any stand-up comic. Don't be afraid to share even your corniest jokes with your child; chances are he'll find them hilarious.

Musical instruments. Banging on a xylophone and chanting, enjoying the rhythmic beat of a drum, making the cymbals clang: a child can become as immersed in musical sound as a Tibetan monk with cymbals. Offer toy instruments with a pleasing sound—recorder, penny whistle, drum, tambourine, electronic keyboard—or allow your child to "play" the piano if you have one. If you enjoy singing, don't be shy about doing it when your child is around, no matter how uninspiring *you* think your voice is; she will take enormous pleasure in chiming in.

> *Make a joyful noise to the LORD, all the earth;*
> *break forth into joyous song and sing praises!*
> *Sing praises to the LORD with the lyre,*
> *with the lyre and the sound of melody!*
> *With trumpets and the sound of the horn*
> *make a joyful noise before the*
> *King, the LORD!*
>
> *—Psalm 98*

Other imaginative toys. Any plaything that lets the imagination soar, from a kite to a swing to a rocking horse to building blocks, helps keep the child open to discover prayer, by helping her to know moments of joyous connection, of resting in the larger, spiritual reality, which prefigure adult prayer.

Silence and guided imagery. Many young children are comfortable with brief periods of silence, and for adults who are not comfortable with prayer aloud, this is a wonderful way to begin.

> *Be still, and know that I am God.*
> *—Psalm 46:10*

Children as young as three years of age, in some cases, can participate in more structured periods of silent prayer. Choose a time when everyone seems relatively calm, your home is quiet (television off), and you are not about to rush out to do errands or car pool. Find a comfortable place where you can sit to-gether—a sofa is fine, and so is a hammock in the backyard. "Let's have some quiet time for a few minutes," you can suggest. "That can help us calm down and feel God with us. Let's sit here and be quiet until I say *Amen* [or *Peace*, or *Thank you*, or simply, *And let's open our eyes now*]." Holding hands, or sitting close enough so that you touch, adds to the intimacy of the moment. In your early attempts, time the silent period for one minute, then two, then three. You can also end the silence with a favorite verse from a psalm or a poem, with the ringing of a small bell, with singing, or with some recorded music.

If children are not able to stop giggling and squirming on a particular day, there is no need to scold. Instead, we can express regret that they have missed out on a special privilege. "I guess we missed our chance today," we can say. "But there will be other times."

If you have trouble finding the "right" time for a period of silence like this, try a moment of silence before dinner. One three-year-old girl I know regularly sits down and tells her parents and older brother in a voice of quiet authority, "Let's do the quiet grace. Everybody *be quiet*."

Silence can be a lovely part of a child's bedtime ritual. After reading a story, suggest a few moments of quiet together before you say good night. One mother concludes these moments by singing Brahms's "Lullabye" to her son and daughter each night.

Many children are remarkably responsive to the use of *guided imagery*, which is the use of verbal "exercises" to help tune out distractions, relax body and mind, and allow the imagination to open to deeper spiritual awareness. Earlier chapters included some simple breathing and centering exercises for parents. If your child is an infant or toddler, hold her in your lap during these relaxation periods, and rub her back soothingly as she shares the peace.

. . . Play Is a Child's Prayer

With a child who is three or older, you may feel comfortable introducing these exercises once you have spent several months doing them yourself. Depending on your family's schedule and preferences, choose a time after school, or just before dinner. (The traditional early morning does not seem to suit the average harried family.) Unplug the telephone, and have each member of the family choose a comfortable pillow on which to sit cross-legged, or lie down. (If your child is young, you both may prefer to hold her in your lap.) Some children find it soothing to hold a small ball of play dough or clay, or to draw in a circular motion with a crayon on paper.

You will recognize this exercise from chapter 3. There is no need to read it aloud; once you are familiar with doing it yourself, the words come easily. Be brief, and speak in a pleasant relaxed voice.

"Listen to your breathing. Breathe in . . . and . . . out. In . . . and . . . out. Notice the air moving into your nostrils and out again. Keep breathing, slowly, in . . . and . . . out . . . If you notice any thoughts, or worries, just let . . . them . . . go."

Pause. Now guide the child's attention to various parts of her body, directing her to tighten the muscles in each area and then relax them. Start with the legs and move upward, to the stomach, chest, arms and hands, mouth, and forehead. "Pay attention to your legs. Notice how they feel. Breathe in, and squeeze the muscles in your legs. Hold the squeeze. Now breathe out, and let go . . . feel your legs relax."

At our house, silence is often introduced when bickering begins. In the winter, the children are sent off to their rooms for quiet time "until they feel peaceful again." In the summer, when the children are arguing over the sharing of toys in the sandbox and I realize I am feeling as cranky as they sound, I announce (as calmly as I can) a walk to the pond for quiet time. They always resist, of course. But after a few minutes of gazing at the water that seems to reflect the whole sky, together we seem to rediscover that our own lives can mirror a reality larger than our petty concerns. Peaceful once more, they return to play, and to resolving their conflicts more calmly.

Spoken prayer. The way to begin to pray with your child is with the way *you* feel comfortable doing it. Time together praying aloud is valuable when our children sense that we are, on some level, open to it. This does not mean we need to feign the pushiness of a TV preacher. We do need to find a way that we can offer our child as simply and naturally as we would a bowl of soup on a winter's day.

What probably makes parents most *un*comfortable about praying aloud with children is the fear that they will *ask* for things. "Prayer as giving thanks, yes," said one father of two flatly. "As asking for things, no." Will Sarah get a new bicycle by asking God for one? Will Grandpa get better if we pray for him? Perhaps you remember Huckleberry Finn's "prayer lesson" from Miss Watson. It turns him into a skeptic.

> She told me to pray every day, and whatever I asked for I would get it. But it warn't so. I tried it. Once I got a fish-line, but no hooks. It warn't any good to me without hooks. I tried for the hooks three or four times, but somehow I couldn't make it work. . . . I set down, one time, back in the woods, and had a long think about it. . . . No, says I to myself, there ain't nothing in it.

Turning prayer into requests for supernatural signs, for drastic action on God's part, seems to suggest that God is only active when extraordinary miracles occur. Yet as we encourage our children to pray, we can help them understand that answers to prayer most often come in the form of everyday miracles. God makes gardens grow, to use an obvious example, when we plant the seeds and water them.

In any case, although we tend to picture a child praying aloud as one who is asking God for things as though she were ordering a kid's meal in a box at McDonald's, in reality *thanksgiving*, and not "petitionary" prayer (asking for things), is the child's spontaneous mode of expression. Some of the most sensitive insights into children's prayer come from the Italian Montessori educator Sofia Cavalletti. "The prayer of children up to the age of seven or eight is almost exclusively prayer of thanksgiving and praise," writes Cavalletti. In *The Religious Potential of the Child*, the book in which she describes her twenty-five years of working with groups of children from the ages of three to eleven in Montessori children's houses, Cavalletti is practically militant about the inappropriateness of teaching petitionary prayer. "The adult who tries to lead the child to prayers of petition *falsifies* and *distorts* the child's religious expression," she warns. "The child feels no need to ask because he knows himself to be in the peaceful possession of certain goods."

For the young child, giving thanks is an expression of the basic trust which, as we saw in the previous chapter, characterizes earliest faith development. "Thank you for my mommy, my daddy, my dolly, and myself," said a four-year-old girl. A six-year-old who worried that his prayers were getting too long-winded decided to sum them up: "Thank you for the entire universe."

Many parents introduce spoken prayer at mealtime. We may begin by simply expressing our thanks for the food we are about to eat. Young children join in saying grace with great gusto, arguing over whose turn comes first, how everyone's hands should be folded, and exactly what to say ("You forgot to thank God for having *me* as your brother, dummy!"). If the "discussion" is getting disruptive, offer quiet reassurance: "The important thing is not the way we sit, or the exact words that we say," we can explain. "These are just ways we let our bodies relax so we can think about our day and feel God is with us."

> *God is great,*
> *God is good,*
> *Let us thank Him for our food.*
> *Amen.*

Bedtime, when we feel relaxed and close, is another opportunity. "I prefer to say bedtime prayers with my kids," said one father of three boys, "because my wife is not really comfortable with praying aloud, and I don't want to put her on the spot by trying to make it part of mealtime." Consider a few moments of sharing the events of the day: What happened that was special today? What didn't go so well? How might I act differently if I had the same problem another time? Our purpose during this time is not to offer pep talks or advice, but to be supportive as our child learns to reflect on her own life.

If a child is afraid of the dark, praying together can be reassuring. Remind her that she sleeps surrounded by the love of her whole family, Mommy and Daddy and Grandma and Grandpa and so on, with God loving us all.

. . . Play Is a Child's Prayer

> *I turned the gas down, I got into bed. I said some words
> to the close and holy darkness, and then I slept.*
> —A Child's Christmas in Wales, *Dylan Thomas*

If you would prefer *not* to make up your own words, there
are many ways to share traditional prayers.

- Read a page from a book of children's prayers (see appendix
  and boxes throughout this section), or sing a simple hymn
  together ("Amazing Grace," "Kum-ba-ya," etc.). Collect favorite prayers (traditional or made up by members of your
  family) in a loose-leaf notebook.

- Read a *single* verse of a psalm or a *single* line from a poem
  such as the Lord's Prayer. For example, teach your child to
  say "The Lord is my shepherd, I shall not want," from the
  Twenty-third Psalm, and allow her to repeat it as she likes.
  You might even provide a tiny lamb, or shepherd and sheep
  figures from a toy farm set. Using abbreviated versions of
  well-known prayers this way helps her give expression to her
  own spirituality rather than encouraging her to learn her own
  garbled versions of them.

- Share different names for God with your child, and simply
  allow her to repeat them: Prince of Peace, Great Spirit, Holy
  One. With each name, her ability to imagine the divine is
  enriched, just as the Hindus understand in their practice of
  reciting "the thousand names for God." "No name of God
  can really describe everything that God is," one mother explained, as she taught her children that God is sometimes
  called "mother." "People have been trying for thousands of

years to think of different names that will help us begin to describe God."

Names for God

Here are some images of God drawn from the Psalms. When the moment feels right, ask your child, "If God were a castle, what would he be like?" If she is responsive to the image, she may wish to talk about it, or draw a picture.

shepherd	son
great bird	lantern
strong tower	friend
sun	light
father	shield
mother	castle
protecting bird	king
rock	helper

Prayer rituals often seem to develop naturally, out of each family's routine and temperaments. One mother takes her seven-year-old daughter in her arms each day before she leaves for school and prays for blessings on the child all through the day. "I think it gives *both* of us a sense that God is with her," says the mother. "And when I forget, she always reminds me!"

Another mother murmurs "Peace" in her child's ear as she hugs him before she drops him off at nursery school.

And another offers her son an age-old parting phrase each morning as he ran out to the school bus: "Remember who you are!" One morning she forgot. As the little boy was halfway across the lawn, he turned around and called out over his shoulder, "Remember who I am!"

A father who feels uncomfortable with formal prayer makes a point of thanking God for things in the time he spends with his children. "We say we're thankful for them, for our health, for loving one another," he says. "I may never manage to bring myself to bow my head with them, but I don't want them to take life for granted."

We can share our awareness of the blessings in our lives by telling our children how thankful we are that Grandma is feeling better, that we have an opportunity to help out at a local thrift shop, that towns all over our state have begun recycling.

If we are really uncomfortable with praying aloud, there are other ways to begin to enjoy moments of sharing God's presence. Why not let our child take the lead? "What do you feel happy about today?" we might ask. "What would you like to say thank-you to God for?" Then, as the child offers a list of thank-you's—not only for favorite toys, but for Mommy and Daddy—we feel the overflowing of love that is the divine presence in our midst.

In time, we may even feel comfortable joining in, however tentatively. "I prayed this morning, for the first time in years," said one mother of a boy and girl, ages eight and four. She sounded surprised. "I just decided to say, 'Well, God, I'm here.'" She smiled hesitantly. "It felt good."

Lord of Creation! I do not know how to pray; I do not know what to say—I give Thee the entire prayer book.
—Hasidic prayer

8. Children and Our Sacred Earth

"And you really live by the river? What a jolly life!"

"By it and with it and on it and in it," said the Rat. *"It's a brother and sister to me, and aunts, and company, and food and drink, and (naturally) washing. It's my world, and I don't want any other."*

—*THE WIND IN THE WILLOWS,*
KENNETH GRAHAME

Every other Saturday Rob and seven-year-old Tony spend a few hours at a nature center near home, caring for small animals in outdoor cages. They like to play with the rabbits and snakes. In his pocket Tony brings along a jackknife, which he uses to chop up carrots and apples for the turtles. Sometimes the two of them clean out the cages. Although Rob and his family attend church every Sunday, he's not sure he sees a connection between religion and his time with Tony at the nature center. "I'm not going to tell you we see rainbows or stars in the sky," says Rob with a friendly laugh. "Tony likes being intimate with the animals and holding them—they're kind of helpless. We feel a closeness, a friendliness. It's a nice father-son outing."

Rob's reluctance to describe his visits to the nature center as "spiritual" reflects some of the problems with much of Western spiritual teaching about nature. Historically speaking, our Judeo-Christian traditions (unlike those of Native Americans and others) have been widely interpreted for the benefit of the *human* species. According to this view, the natural world was created for human use, as a source of our food, shelter, and clothing. "The creatures were not made for themselves," declared one Jacobean bishop, "but for the use and service of man." Any "spirituality" of nature was limited, for the most part, to isolated moments of poetic inspiration praising its beauty—the awe-filled visions of "rainbows" and "stars" Rob has some doubts about.

Yet with the proliferation of air and water pollution and toxic wastes, we are beginning to recognize how much damage this human-centered worldview has done to our planet. We are understanding that our *total* relationship with the environment, our bonds with all creatures, are profoundly spiritual.

"Love of nature is not about just standing under the stars and saying 'Oh,' " said one mother flatly.

Love of nature is our awareness that we are inextricably linked with all life. Like all spirituality, it is reflected in little things: in the foods we eat, the materials we use to package our merchandise, the way we dispose of our garbage.

"The natural world is the larger sacred community to which we belong," the ecologist and theologian Thomas Berry has said. "To be alienated from this community is to become destitute in all that makes us human. To damage this community is to diminish our own existence." If we understand spirituality as an awareness of our sacred connections with *all* life, then authentic spiritual nurture is concerned with a child's bonds with *all* living creatures.

An Astronaut's View

The Earth reminded us of a Christmas tree ornament hanging in the blackness of space. As we got farther and farther away it diminished in size. Finally it shrank to the size of a marble, the most beautiful marble you can imagine. That beautiful, warm, living object looked so fragile, so delicate, that if you touched it with a finger it would crumble and fall apart. Seeing this has to change a man, has to make a man appreciate the creation of God and the love of God.
—James Irwin, who spent twelve days in space in 1971
(from The Home Planet *by Kevin W. Kelley)*

Of course, we help our child come to recognize the natural world as an abundant source of blessing: of air, food, and water. But we also encourage her to know and honor her relatedness to other living creatures by teaching her how we protect the earth and its resources, a concept expressed in the Bible as our *stewardship* of creation. The earth does not belong to us; we are its caretakers, or "stewards." These lessons are usually simple and low-key, like the hours of love and care Rob and Tony share at the nature center.

Something More...

"I tell my kids we don't waste water or electricity, because it's not fair, because we want to preserve our resources," said one mother of two school-age children. "I guess when you think about it, that's a profoundly spiritual notion." Through spiritual nurture we can help our children know our sacred earth the way the Rat in *The Wind in the Willows* knows his beloved river— as a "a brother and sister to me, and aunts, and company, and food and drink, and (naturally) washing."

Most of the time, without realizing it, we tend to teach our children about the earth as though it were no more than a giant storehouse created for our use. Cows give milk, we tell them. Chickens lay eggs. Sheep give wool. We need to save water or we won't have enough. We do need to speak with our children in concrete terms, of course, because they learn through their senses. And they, being naturally egocentric, lap up the idea that the earth's creatures exist for their benefit; don't the sun and moon follow them everywhere? But just as we seek to avoid presenting religious doctrine and stories which we know they are bound to distort because of their limited cognitive abilities, we can help them transcend their egocentric view of the natural world.

We do this by nurturing their inborn sense of *kinship* with other living creatures. They love nothing better than feeding the ducks in the park. They talk to squirrels. "Does it hurt the trees when the leaves fall off?" inquired a two-and-a-half-year-old girl.

"*P*retty crummy it rained on my birthday," grumbled a boy holding his mother's hand in a supermarket parking lot. He looked five or six. Pouting slightly, he reached up and pulled on the hood of his jacket.

"Why do you say that?" replied his mother in a cheerful tone. "Imagine all the plants getting a good drink on your birthday."

The boy's eyes lit up. "Yeah, I guess that's a *really* happy birthday," he said, smiling.

As we help our child deepen this intimate way of relating to other living creatures, we see her grow into the role of a *steward*, or protector and caretaker. Have you ever met a child who would let a bird feeder hang empty? One day as I was eating lunch with my four-year-old son in an overcrowded ski lodge, he gazed out the window at the mountain and confided in a dreamy voice, "You know what I love about nature? It's sooo-o-o quiet. It's not like being in here, with lots of people going bla-bla-bla. It's peaceful. It's calm." He paused in silent contemplation as he popped a french fry into his mouth. "It makes me feel like . . . like a park ranger!"

Albert Schweitzer once wrote that as a small child, he could not understand why in his evening prayers he should pray for human beings only. "So when my mother had prayed with me and had kissed me goodnight, I used to add silently a prayer that I had composed myself for all living creatures," he recalled. "It ran thus: 'O heavenly Father, protect and bless all things that have breath; guard them from all evil and let them sleep in peace.' "

> Absorbed in the new life he was entering upon, intoxicated with the sparkle, the ripple, the scents and the sounds and the sunlight, he trailed a paw in the water and dreamed long waking dreams.

Many parents worry that we cannot teach our child about the natural world because we don't know much about it ourselves.

Something More...

We have trouble distinguishing a song sparrow from a wood-pecker. We can't tell a sugar maple from a swamp maple. But deepening our child's awareness of her bonds with other creatures is not a matter of dragging her along on purposeful hikes to stalk out twenty species of plants and collect their leaves for display in a specimen box. Nor is it teaching her to memorize the names and dietary preferences of twelve different dinosaurs. Facts alone cannot be the basis of a living connection with the earth. Facts offer nothing more than the books Dylan Thomas remembered receiving as gifts, as he wrote in *A Child's Christmas in Wales*—books that "told me everything about the wasp, except why."

For the purposes of spiritual nurture, the information we share about each life form is not intended to define it, but to help our children *see* it more clearly. We seek to find out about other creatures just as we are eager to learn absolutely everything about someone we are growing to love. We seek to discover the infinite variety of creation because each discovery tells us something more about the Creator. God wrote two books, said St. Augustine: the Bible and nature. ("I like the nature book better," commented one five-year-old in no uncertain terms.)

And as nature guides have always told us, the most vivid lessons come through direct encounters. A child remembers that which she has touched and tasted and smelled. In the spring, she breathes in the scent of lilacs beside the front door. At the beach she runs her fingers through the water and licks the salt on them. In the fall she watches the leaves drop into red and gold piles.

Liz, a reporter, was surprised by her four-year-old daughter Marcy's fear of a centipede in the driveway. "I talked with her about how everybody has a place in the universe," Liz said. "I told her, 'There is a place for the bug and for you, and we don't step on that bug or smash it because we're all part of the same chain.' " So vividly did Marcy remember those words that now she refuses to let anyone even squash a spider in the bathroom; it must be gingerly picked up and carried outside.

> Long ago, in Kentucky, I, a boy, stood
> By a dirt road, in first dark, and heard
> The great geese hoot northward.
> I could not see them, there being no moon
> and the stars sparse. I heard them.
> I did not know what was happening in my heart.
> —*From* Audubon: A Vision,
> Robert Penn Warren

At a surprisingly early age, children also seem to experience moments of overwhelming oneness with the world around them, moments that fill them with a sense of peace and awe that lingers for a lifetime. Many of us remember times like these from our own childhoods. "One of my first spiritual experiences was staring out a window at a bunch of trees, and just feeling an incredible peace come over me," said Liz.

One of the mothers I interviewed remembered sitting beside a lake for hours with her son when he was no older than eighteen months. "He'd be in my lap, and the two of us would just sit and stare at the water," she said quietly. "We'd watch the reflections of the tree branches on the surface of the water. We'd be perfectly silent for an hour or two. Those were precious times." Her words reminded me of *The Wind in the Willows* and of Mole, who "trailed a paw in the water and dreamed long waking dreams."

In *The Irrational Season*, Madeleine L'Engle recalls a night when, as a baby on a visit to her grandmother's home in Florida, she was picked up out of the crib and carried outdoors for her first look at the stars. "The night sky, the constant rolling of breakers against the shore, the stupendous light of the stars, all made an indelible impression on me," she writes.

> I was intuitively aware not only of a beauty I had never seen before but also that the world was far greater than the protected limits of the small child's world which was all that I had known thus far. . . . I had been taught to say my prayers at night: Our Father, and a long string of God-blesses, and it was that first showing of the galaxies which gave me an awareness that the God I spoke to at bedtime was extraordinary and not just a bigger and better combination of the grown-up powers of my mother and father.

Brief though they usually are, encounters like these plant a seed in a child's heart. They impart a sense of her own place on the earth, and in the universe beyond, which she will not be able to grasp with her logical faculties for many years to come. "A single glimpse of heaven is enough to confirm its existence," wrote Abraham Maslow, "even if it is never experienced again."

People in ancient cultures have long known this, of course. Do you remember the naming ceremony depicted in Alex Haley's *Roots?* The father Omoro carried eight-day-old Kunta Kinte alone out under the moon and stars. He lifts his baby up with his face to the heavens and says softly, "Behold—the only thing greater than yourself."

✳   ✳   ✳

Introduction of the Child to the Cosmos

Ho! Ye Sun, Moon, Stars, all ye that move in the
      heavens,
I bid you hear me! Into your midst has come a new
      life.
  Consent ye, I implore! Make its path smooth,
  that it may reach the brow of the first hill.
Ho! Ye Winds, Clouds, Rain, all ye that move in the
      air,
I bid you hear me! Into your midst has come a new
      life.
  Consent ye, I implore! Make its path smooth,
  that it may reach the brow of the second hill.
Ho! Ye Hills, Rivers, Trees, all ye of the earth,
I bid you hear me! Into your midst has come a new
      life.
  Consent ye, I implore! Make its path smooth,
  that it may reach the brow of the third hill.
Ho! Ye Birds, great and small, that fly in the air,
Ho! Ye Animals, great and small, that dwell in the
      forest,
Ho! Ye Insects that creep among the grasses,
I bid you hear me! Into your midst has come a new
      life.
  Consent ye all, I implore! Make its path smooth,
  that it may reach the brow of the fourth hill.
Ho! All ye of the heavens, all ye of the air,

171

> all ye of the earth; I bid you all to hear me!
> Into your midst has come a new life. Consent ye, I
>   implore!
> Make its path smooth—then shall it travel beyond the
>   four hills.
>
> —Omaha people

He learnt to swim and to row, and entered into the joy of running water; and with his ear to the reed-stems he caught, at intervals, something of what the wind went whispering so constantly among them.

*H*elping our child grow closer to other living creatures does not require a naturalist's expertise or a hiker's stamina. We acquaint our child with the natural world just as we would introduce her to an old friend. We will be more relaxed if we do not expect every moment to be pure pleasure, however. Take a child along on a picnic and you are likely to hear that the bugs are biting, the grass is damp, and the sun is in her eyes.

One family rented a Winnebago to drive their three boys across the Canadian Rockies. "All we heard was how bumpy the ride was," grumbled the mother.

We need to choose our moment, to accept the fact that often they feel more like frolicking than enjoying the scenery. And sometimes they even feel like bickering.

But then—perhaps when we least expect it—they stop, like Mole (who discovers life on the river and the joy of running water), to catch something of what the wind whispers among the reed-stems.

Here are some ways parents can help that happen.

Help your child grow attentive. "Only children can hear the song of the male house mouse," Annie Dillard has written. "Only children keep their eyes open." Often our child's eagerness for encounters with nature seems to come at the most inconvenient times.

We are outside catching our death of cold, and she insists on pulling off her mittens to examine a pine cone. "Look, Mom, it has a sticky part," she says, fingering the sap. "And it smells like a Christmas tree."

When we greet the earth and its creatures with open hearts, we are likely to have some surprising encounters, even though we may be the most inexpert of naturalists. Next to the pond behind our house there are rabbits living in the bramble bushes. One afternoon I carried my two-year-old son out toward the wooden baby swing that hangs from an oak branch. Suddenly I spotted a rabbit some ten feet away. "Look," I whispered, pointing. The rabbit, small and brown, hopped right up to us and sat at my feet, staring. Together the three of us waited in hushed silence.

As we grow to understand that our child's spiritual connection with nature grows through simple encounters such as these, we find it easier to set aside time for them. With a *young child*, we need "do" very little. We hold our infant up to rub the rough bark of a tree with her fingers.

We sit quietly with a preschooler at the foot of a tree and listen for woodpeckers.

We stop to watch an earthworm in a puddle on the driveway after a storm.

We lie on our backs together and stare up at the clouds;

as our child imagines the clouds as animals or angels chasing each other across the blue, we notice how different the trees look from this angle.

We listen to the birds and the wind. We smell the sweet, fresh-cut grass.

With a child over the age of *four*, we can go on what the nature educator Joseph Cornell calls a "micro-hike," with a piece of string about a yard long, and a magnifying glass. Take the string and stretch it out along the ground. Lie facedown next to your child. Now use the magnifying glass to take a close-up look at the soil, the blades of grass, the rocks that look like mountains, the ants and spiders—everything along the length of string.

By the time a child is *five or six* she may prefer more active encounters, such as running through the woods playing Tarzan or Robin Hood. "If I begin to wax rhapsodic about nature and life, my kids begin to hum and sing and talk about cartoons," one mother of two school-age children admitted. "I lose them unless I keep it simple. We might look at the moss on a rock, or watch an anthill. The *most* I might say is, 'Isn't it interesting that God made the world like this?' "

At this stage attentiveness can be nurtured through close observation, as the child's propensity to wonder takes an analytical turn. One mother who had always been touched by her son's love of animals recalled the day his pet manta died. "I thought it would be a tragedy. I was ready to stage an elaborate funeral," she said. Without shedding a tear, the six-year-old asked to borrow a pair of rubber gloves and a knife. He plucked the fish out of the tank, carried it into the bathroom, and lopped off its head. "Look, Mom," he exclaimed, "I found the brains!"

As a child learns to write, she may enjoy walking around the yard or park with a pad of paper, making lists of "signs of spring" or "places wildflowers are growing."

Many school-age children are responsive to the idea of

"training" as nature guides in the Native American tradition. In Forrest Carter's autobiographical *The Education of Little Tree*, the story of a Cherokee boyhood of the 1930s, Little Tree describes his first walk on the high trail in the boot moccasins his grandmother had made for him:

> I trotted behind Granpa and I could feel the upward slant of the trail. I could feel something more, as Granma said I would. Mon-o-lah, the earth mother, came to me through my moccasins. I could feel her push and swell here, and sway and give there . . . and the roots that veined her body and the life of the water-blood, deep inside her. She was warm and springy and bounced me on her breast, as Granma said she would.

We can invite our small "scout" to slip on a pair of moccasins or socks and tread quietly in the woods. Together, we feel the earth under our feet, and listen carefully for birds and insects.

Go for walks. It is hard to think of a more obvious way to bring our children into contact with the natural world. And yet walks with children can be discouraging. We worry about the traffic. We don't get any exercise because they walk so slowly. They dawdle. They get tired and ask to be carried, or they want to turn back before we've gone ten feet. "We're not about to climb to deserted mountain meadows in order to commune with the purity of nature," said one mother firmly.

One solution is to avoid long-distance hikes until the children are older, at least. "We had a great time taking a slow walk around the backyard," commented one father during a February thaw. "We looked at all the little shoots just starting to poke up out of the ground." Taking regular walks along the same route, rather than aiming for constant trailblazing, has its advantages. You get to know the lay of the land and to recognize the plants and animals that inhabit it. You notice small changes. You get a sense of *place.*

Every day for two years we visited a small waterfall that runs off a stream not far from our house. One March afternoon we found the water pounding on the rocks and splashing the branches that had collected at the bottom. "Why is the water falling so hard?" the children asked.

The snow had melted at the top of the hill, I explained, and was draining off. Over the next few days we talked about how snow melts on mountains and flows into rivers. By Thanksgiving they were fascinated to see that the "water fountain," as the two-year-old called it, had frozen into a solid, rippled sheet. Our small corner of the world was beginning to fit into the changing climate beyond the neighborhood.

Walking a regular route together, we also come to appreciate the variety of the seasons, of course, and the gifts each one brings. One mother remembered learning this way on long walks with her grandmother, an immigrant from southern Italy. "During good weather, we would forage for mushrooms in the woods. We would find wild grapes. We knew when things were growing, when they were coming into season, where to go for them, how they grew," she recalled. "At least my grandmother knew, and through her I was learning."

Night walks are a special thrill for kids of all ages. Winter is a good time, because the sky is clear and darkness falls well before a child's bedtime. (Check with the newspaper to find out when the moon will be full, and wear warm clothing.) The last thing most of us feel like doing after a busy day is bundling up the children and traipsing around outdoors, but standing under the stars together has a way of broadening our perspective. For inspiration, read Frances Hamerstrom's *Walk When the Moon Is Full.*

> *I see the moon,*
> *And the moon sees me;*
> *God bless the moon,*
> *And God bless me.*

If you live in an area where you are not at risk of Lyme disease, or are visiting one, bring your child on a *barefoot walk*. Teach her how to take slow, short steps, avoiding leaves or twigs underfoot, so that she can walk silently and listen for animals.

Catch the wind. Buy a baby or toddler a pinwheel. Hang a brightly colored wind sock or pretty wind chime near her window.

Help your preschooler or school-age child make a mobile. You will need construction paper, fine thread, and three- or four-inch pieces of thin wire in graduated lengths (cut sections from wire coat hangers work well). Draw or trace shapes (fish, butterflies, birds, etc.) on the construction paper, then tape them to short lengths of fine thread. Now tie one hanging shape to either end of each piece of thin wire. Tie each rod to a slightly longer rod until you have assembled the mobile.

With an older child, fly a kite. Make your own, or buy a simple kite with a tail. Holding on to the string and running as the kite soars is a living lesson in working with natural forces, in this case the wind. (Children over six enjoy making kites as well as flying them; younger kids tend to lack the patience and coordination to keep track of the string while running.)

Play "Guess What I Am?" Children as young as four

enjoy playing animal or plant guessing games. Each player supplies a clue ("I have eight legs," a young child pretending to be a spider might say), or does an imitation with sound effects, until someone guesses the right answer. Older children can check a nature encyclopedia or magazine for more sophisticated clues. As with all nature fantasy games and activities, this is a simple way of helping a child relate to the natural world with playfulness and imagination.

Use simple guided imagery to bring a child closer to the natural world. Beginning with the breathing exercise on page 56, encourage your child to imagine herself as her favorite animal, or as a tree, or an underwater creature. As she closes her eyes, invite her to explore her native habitat with all her senses, find food, meet friendly animals, experience different seasons. If she is a tree or flower, she can "drink" up water and nutrients through her roots, feel the warmth of the sun on her leaves, and notice seasonal changes (including snow and rain as well as animal friends). Younger children often enjoy responding to imagery through movement and dance. You may wish to play a recording of Vivaldi's *The Four Seasons*.

Put up a bird feeder. One mother was sitting at the kitchen table making up a grocery list. "Let's see, what do we need?" she murmured. "Milk, eggs . . ."

"And don't forget birdseed!" her three-year-old daughter interjected. The birds had become part of the family.

It's hard to imagine a better microcosm of the natural world than a bird feeder. Children quickly grow familiar with the various local species, notice their different bills and tails, and begin to distinguish male from female. Perhaps most important, they discover how, during the winter months, the birds come to depend on the food we provide. Young children enjoy making their own bird feeder by spreading a pine cone with peanut butter and hanging it from a tree.

Make your yard a wildlife refuge. We try to teach our children to relate to animals, and then what do we do? We put up fencing to keep out deer and buy trash cans with raccoon-proof lids. With minimal effort, we can attract *friendly* wildlife to the backyard and enjoy watching it with children of all ages. Birds love berry bushes and seeds. We can leave a hollow log on the ground for birds to nest in, or nail a nesting box to the south side of a tree.

Butterflies are attracted to brightly colored flowers.

Small animals come to visit a brush pile made of branches and bushes they can hide under.

Garden together. "Gardening is an active participation in the deepest mysteries of the universe," writes Thomas Berry. "By gardening our children learn that they constitute with all growing things a single community of life." Preparing the beds, watering seedlings, learning how to fertilize the plants and control the weeds without harming the soil: all these are simple, time-honored ways of relating to the natural world. Day by day they help us build a sense of closeness and caring and teach us the meaning of stewardship.

"In the summer every night after supper," said a father who is an attorney, "my seven-year-old son and I are out in the garden together on our hands and knees, planting seeds, weeding, watering."

"We're gardeners," said a mother of two. "We're not *good* gardeners. We grow flowers because we don't have any place in the yard that's sunny enough for vegetables. But the kids have their own small patch."

Kids can help start a compost heap out of non-meat kitchen scraps and garden materials. Set aside a special bin in the kitchen for their apple cores, bread crusts, and so on. They can help carry it out to the garden on a regular basis (simply make a heap, or enclose it in chicken wire). Add leaves, soil, grass clippings, and alfalfa meal or other organic fertilizer, and turn the heap with a pitchfork once in a while. Be sure to warn your child that the compost is hot to the touch; if she is six or seven or older she will be interested in learning that the heap is a home for decay-causing bacteria that are turning your garbage into food for new plants.

If you have no space at all for a garden, try container planting. And houseplants and herbs in pots offer opportunities for watering, feeding, and tender care all year round.

Share seasonal cooking. Buying or picking local fruits and vegetables is a vivid lesson in our interdependence with nature and one that indigenous creatures have never forgotten. When we cook foods that are in season, we recognize our dependence on the earth. Sweet foods are always popular with kids, of course: apricots in the spring, berries and berry short-cakes and cobblers in summertime, apples or apple pie in the fall, and pancakes with maple syrup in the winter. Check with your newspaper to see if you and your child can pick your own produce at a local farm or orchard or plan to see a maple sugaring demonstration at a nature center.

Talk about garbage. There is no such thing as throwing anything "away." Garbage is always with us. We can tell our children that according to the United Nations Environmental Programme, each person in the United States generates nearly a *ton* of trash every year (half the weight of a small car). We can educate our children and encourage them to join us in cutting our family's garbage production in a variety of ways:

- cutting down on use of paper cups and plates
- making regular visits to our local recycling center, or writing a letter to local government requesting that one be established. "The kids are in charge of putting cans in a bag and helping

us redeem them at the supermarket," said one mother of two girls, ages four and five. "They get to keep the money, which pleases them no end."

- asking for recycled paper at the stationery store; drawing on the front *and* back of paper
- refusing unneeded paper or plastic bags in stores

These small measures do not in themselves turn us or our children into "more spiritual" people. Yet when they reflect an awareness of our sacred connections with the earth and its creatures, they can be everyday "sacraments" of sorts.

Help your child learn to choose toys that last. Children are bombarded by television commercials touting highly breakable plastic toys that quickly end up in the garbage—wasting the resources used to make them, and adding to the earth's waste-disposal problem.

We can help our children learn that buying a well-made toy that lasts is one way of expressing love for the earth and conserving resources. Another way is by giving them some toys that have been handed down by older friends or cousins. A trip to a museum or local historical society is often an opportunity to see toys—wooden tops and hoops, for example—that have been around for generations or even millennia. Shops that sell antiques and collectibles often yield surprising treasures: old wooden boats, for example, and wonderful toy fire engines. Even simpler, ask your kids to explore their rooms and find toys that seem sturdy enough to be handed down to their own children one day—with no missing parts.

And when a school-age child begs for the latest trendy toy, we can ask her to consider two questions: (1) Is it breakable (lots of small plastic parts), or is it made to last? (2) How long will I enjoy playing with it?

Use earth-loving art supplies. Recycled household materials—pieces of fabric, yogurt containers, egg cartons, frozen-dinner containers, ice-pop sticks, toilet-paper rolls—make wonderful homemade puppets, swords, and dolls. As you're shopping in the supermarket or cooking dinner, ask kids to keep track of packaging that can be saved for art projects. Collages of natural backyard materials offer endless possibilities.

School-age children enjoy experimenting with natural dyes and stains. Boil six loose handfuls of onion skins in a two-quart enameled saucepan filled with water. Strain out the onion skins and reserve the liquid. Pour the homemade dye bath back into the saucepan, and put in some clean, white cotton fabric. Simmer, stirring with a wooden spoon, until the fabric is bright yellow. You can also dye paper by dipping it into the dye bath and then patting it dry. To dye fabric green, use spinach cooking water. Blackberries yield a nice blue, and coffee grounds make brown. (Since these colors are not fixed, however, the dyed fabrics are not washable.)

Tell the stories of lovers of the natural world. Johnny Appleseed, John Muir, George Washington Carver, Saint Francis of Assisi, Mary Leakey, Henry David Thoreau, John James Audubon, Jane Goodall: the biographies of these and lesser-known people who have lived close to the land can be exciting and inspiring to children.

Teach your child to be an "ecology detective." In a variety of fun ways we can help increase our children's awareness of the many small things we can do each day to protect our sacred earth.

Starting when they are four or five, we can help them become aware of the overpackaging of food and merchandise. In the supermarket, they can learn to choose cereal and cookies in boxes made of recycled cardboard (gray on the inside). We can show them that we choose eggs packed in cardboard cartons rather than Styrofoam ones. We can encourage them to help us pack groceries in reused bags brought from home, or in canvas sacks.

At home, they can watch for leaky faucets and keep doors and windows closed while the heat or air-conditioning is on. They can turn off lights when not in a room.

At the beach or park, we can teach them to put garbage in the trash cans instead of littering.

We can offer resources to feed their interest in the natural world. (*See appendix for books appropriate for various age groups.*)

School-age children often teach their *parents* environmental awareness. At this stage, our at-home lessons in stewardship begin to translate into community-wide and even global concerns. Now we can encourage them by helping them become involved in projects with friends and schoolmates, from community gardening to recycling to bird-watching to writing letters to legislators.

Celebrate the United Nations Environmental Sabbath. Every year, coinciding with World Environment Day (June 5), the United Nations Environmental Programme sponsors a day of rest for the earth. Faith communities around the world—Buddhist, Christian, Hindu, Jewish, Sikh, Moslem, Native American, Quaker and Baha'i—join in prayer, study, and ritual celebrating the human commitment to the earth. As part of this observance, you and your friends or faith community may choose to organize a service, concert, tree-planting ceremony, or clean-up day with children included.

Each year the U.N. Environmental Programme publishes a magazine filled with information and ideas on preserving the environment, as well as prayers, readings, and songs from different faith traditions for Environmental Sabbath celebrations. Many of these are appropriate for children. (*For further infor-*

Something More...

mation, contact the United Nations Environmental Programme listed in the Resources for Further Exploration section in the appendix.)

*L*ike all loving relationships, our bond with the earth is nurtured in many little ways. Together we set aside time to collect newspapers for recycling, remember to turn off the lights when we leave a room, limit our use of unnecessary packaging. Sometimes we walk instead of taking the car. Small efforts at stewardship such as these may not transform the world overnight. But day by day, they remind us that our family home is very much a part of our planetary home, and that we are spiritually connected with all creation.

Teach your children what we have taught our children, that the earth is our mother. Whatever befalls the earth, befalls the children of the earth. . . .

One thing we know, which the white man may one day discover—our God is the same God. You may think now that you own Him as you wish to own our land; but you cannot. He is the God of all *people, and His compassion is equal for all. This earth is precious to God, and to harm the earth is to heap contempt on its Creator. . . .*

So love it as we have loved it. Care for it as we have cared for it. And with all your strength, with all your mind, with all your heart, preserve it for your children, and love . . . as God loves us all.

—Chief Seattle (Suquamish people), 1854

---

9. "Why Does God Make Bad People?" Responding to Hard Questions

 I INES WRITTEN BY A BEAR
OF VERY LITTLE BRAIN

On Monday when the sun is hot
I wonder to myself a lot:
"Now is it true, or is it not,
"That what is which and which is what?"

——*WINNIE-THE-POOH*, A. A. MILNE

"My daughter asked me if Adam and Eve were really alive," said the mother of a curly-haired, blond six-year-old. "I didn't want to say yes, but I was worried that if I said no I'd turn her off to religion. So I told her we'd talk about it later!"

For many parents, children's questions present some of the greatest challenges of spiritual nurture. We long to offer answers that are nothing less than logical, hopeful, and honest. Yet our actual responses seem woefully inadequate. Like Winnie-the-Pooh, we wonder to ourselves a lot.

Something More...

"I talked to the minister of our church about how to answer questions about death and the afterlife," said a mother of three small children. "He said we're not fundamentalists, so we don't have pat answers to everything. I'm *glad* that's his perspective, and I agree with him. But when I'm trying to come up with an intelligent answer to my five-year-old's questions, it can be frustrating."

At one time or another, most of us resort to delaying tactics. "Changing the subject is my main religious-education technique," said the father of a seven-year-old with a grin. "Yesterday Michael asked me if God made hell. I thought about that one for a minute. Then I said, 'Why don't we kick around the soccer ball for a while until dinnertime, and then you can ask Mom.'"

But delaying tactics don't often work when our child's questions strike close to home. "When we're stepping over homeless people on the sidewalk, it's pretty hard to pretend they're not there," said one mother. "My kids want explanations." Just as we wish we could isolate them forever from uncertainty, pain, and death, we yearn to tie up all the loose ends to their questions. Instead, we seem to be at a loss for words.

Or are we? Perhaps we can begin to think of our silence as something other than a sign that we are incapable of responding to our children's questions.

Paradoxically, it is when we are empty-handed that we have the most to offer. As always on the spiritual journey, realizing we do not have all the answers—or that a quick response is inadequate—is not cause for alarm.

It is the beginning of wisdom. Faced with questions philosophers and theologians have debated for centuries, why do we expect answers to come tripping off our own tongues at the breakfast table?

... "Why Does God Make Bad People?"

In our willingness to wonder, in our awakening to the truth
that we are far from fully understanding life's deepest mysteries,
we open ourselves and our children to growth. "True faith can
only grow and mature if it includes the elements of paradox
and creative doubt," writes the British theologian Kenneth
Leech. "Such doubt is not the enemy of faith but an essential
element within it. For faith in God does not bring the false
peace of answered questions and resolved paradoxes."

> *Leave to your opinions their own quiet undisturbed de-*
> *velopment, which, like all progress, must come from deep*
> *within and cannot be pressed or hurried by anything.*
> Everything *is gestation and then bringing forth.*
> —Rainer Maria Rilke

Some of the wisest reflections on the role of questions in
a child's life are those of the Nobel laureate Elie Wiesel, writing,
in *Night*, of his own childhood musings. "Every question," he
recalls, "possessed a power that did not lie in the answer."
Wiesel remembers Moshe the Beadle, his earliest spiritual guide,
who told him, "Man raises himself toward God by the questions
he asks Him. That is the true dialogue. Man questions God and
God answers. But we don't understand His answers. We can't
understand them."

To this the young Wiesel responds with another question:
"And why do you pray, Moshe?"

The rabbi replies, "I pray to the God within me that He
will give me the strength to ask Him the right questions."

Something More...

Likewise, as spiritual nurturers, we need worry less about providing the "right" answers than about helping our child ask the right questions. Each question he asks is not an impediment to, but a *sign* of, his spiritual growth. Rather than trying to resolve each one, we enable him to struggle and learn for himself. Sometimes we even need to learn when it is best to say nothing at all. And at times, especially as our children approach adolescence, we may realize that answers are more likely to come in conversation with others—peers, a thoughtful teacher, or an approachable member of the clergy, for example.

This does not mean we ought to turn aside from his inquiries, or try to divert him. "If we don't talk about the big issues—hunger, poverty, war," one mother told me, "then our children think we just don't care."

When they bring up painful or difficult subjects, we are supportive in our willingness to face and share their fear and puzzlement, even when we ourselves lack a solution. Admitting that we don't have a good answer to a child's question can be the beginning of a profoundly honest, nurturing exchange. It may serve as an opportunity for us to reevaluate our own assumptions and to consider a challenging issue from a spiritual perspective—perhaps for the first time.

"Why did God make bad people?" asked five-year-old David. His father thought for a moment.

"Well, that's an important question—lots of people have asked it," he began. "A man named Maimonides wrote a very thick book about it."

David's father offered no real "answer." But he had stopped to *listen* to his son. He *affirmed* the importance of David's question. And by mentioning Maimonides he pointed David toward the riches of his faith tradition but avoided complicating the issue with abstract speculation about God's judgment ("Don't worry, all the bad people are going to be punished," etc.). David's father's response was a promising beginning.

To *listening* and *affirming* we might add a third element: a helpful response *invites* further questioning. As we shall see, although we need not offer definitive answers, we can open the window to more ideas by sharing personal experiences and stories handed down through our tradition.

Of the three elements—listening, affirming, and inviting further questions—*listening* is the most important. As we learn to listen with open hearts, we worry less and less about the adequacy of our own explanations. We begin to truly share in our child's process of discovery. Day by day, as we affirm his responses and encourage him to explore, and as we celebrate our lives together, we help him grow in trust, hope, and wisdom. We learn that we need not impose answers on our children, but watch them unfold with time, just as a plant blooms after many waterings.

> "Hallo!" said Piglet, "what are you doing?"
> . . . "Tracking something," said Winnie-the-Pooh very mysteriously.
> "Tracking what?" said Piglet, coming closer.
> "That's just what I ask myself. I ask myself, What?"
> "What do you think you'll answer?"
> "I shall have to wait until I catch up with it," said Winnie-the-Pooh.

No matter how well we think we communicate with our child, something happens the moment he asks a life-and-death question. We panic. "I have difficulty translating concepts into simple language," admitted a mother with three young children. "And I don't feel I have the answers to these questions myself. So when they come up with their zingers, I get a knot in my stomach." We can avoid that sinking feeling when our child comes up with a "zinger" by asking *ourselves* three questions: What is he really asking? How can I respond in a way that will help my child grow? And how can I speak in terms he will understand?

What is my child really asking? As discussed in chapter 6, questions that initially sound like advanced philosophical inquiry are better understood as personal expressions of a child's inner conflicts. When a young child asks a question, Piaget observed, we need to keep in mind that his concern is *functional*, not theoretical. If he asks a question about a murder on the television news, he is not expecting to hear crime statistics or a discussion of capital punishment. He is asking whether the world is a place to be trusted. He wants to know whether the "bad guys" are going to get *him*. When a three-year-old asks, "Why did God make the flood come?" after hearing the story of Noah, he is not grappling in the abstract with the problem of evil. He is looking for reassurance that his home—and Mommy and Daddy and his brother and his precious toys—are not going to end up underwater.

"Sarah's mommy says there's no such thing as God," ventured five-year-old Daniel after school one day as he was building a block tower.

His mother walked over and put her arm around him. "Well, sometimes it doesn't *seem* like God is there, especially when we feel sad," she said in a sympathetic tone. "It *feels* like God must be awfully far away."

Daniel was silent for a moment. "Yeah, well, what do *we* think?" he asked.

. . . "Why Does God Make Bad People?"

"Well," said his mother, bending over to plant a kiss on the top of his head, "when I look at all the wonderful gifts God has given us—the trees, the flowers, each other—I just *know* he's there, even when I'm having a rotten day."

Daniel picked up an oblong block and carefully placed it on top of the tower. "How come Batman doesn't fly?" he asked suddenly. Evidently Daniel's existential crisis had been averted! His mother had realized that he was not looking for a proof of God's existence or an exposition on atheism. He needed to hear that everyone wonders where God is sometimes, and he needed some reassurance.

And when a six-year-old asks, "Is there really a God?" his inquiries reflect his desire for a concrete image of the divine, as well as the fear of death typical of this age.

Six-year-old Jeremy was having a bedtime chat with his mother, who sat beside him on the bed. She had just read him a child's biography of our first president, which Jeremy had thoroughly enjoyed—especially the cherry tree incident. But now Jeremy looked thoughtful. "Why did George Washington die?" he asked.

"Well, he got sick. That happens to people when they get old," said his mother haltingly. "We try to live a full life, and then we die."

He turned toward his mother and hugged her. "I don't want to die," he said. "I don't want *you* to die."

As she hugged him back, she suddenly realized that he had not been asking for an explanation at all. He had, like many six-year-olds, been facing the idea of his own dying. "Everybody in our house is young and healthy, and I don't think we're going to die for a long time," she said softly. "Right now our job is to love each other and learn all we can about the world." Sighing contentedly, Jeremy put his head down on the pillow.

On the other hand, a ten-year-old who says, "*How* can you

think there's a God?" is likely to be expressing his growth beyond the God-image conceptualized within the concrete operational framework of his early school years. Now the man on the cloud seems like a silly, childish idea. In the grown-up world the child is coming to know, love and peace do not seem to emerge victorious. It is time to begin digging deeper, to discuss the ways people have discerned God's moving among us, and to encourage our child to explore the contrast between the biblical vision of creation and the reality of our world.

And once in a while a child comes up with an intimidating question that turns out to be much simpler than it appears. "Why don't some people have houses?" asked my three-year-old daughter one day.

"Well, when apartments cost too much money," I answered carefully, "and people can't earn enough money to pay for them, then they don't have a place to live." I decided to try for a note of hope. "That's why Mommy and Daddy try to help out at the shelter. Daddy reads stories to the kids, and Mommy helps their mommies learn how to take extra-good care of their children while they're staying there."

"Boy, poor people don't know *anything*," Laura concluded.

"Oh, that's not true," I stammered. Of course, my answer had been far too abstract to be understood by a preschooler. It occurred to me that Laura might enjoy actually visiting the shelter on a day when she could join the children at the dining room table for an arts-and-crafts project. I also made a mental note to find a storybook that would offer a view of life beyond our middle-class circle in terms that Laura could understand. Obviously this was a much better approach, but I had a surprise coming.

Two days later Laura asked again, "Mommy, why don't some people have houses?"

"Well, when they're poor they might live in a shelter," I began, intending to invite her on a visit. But she interrupted me.

"No," she said impatiently, "I mean why do some people live in *apartments*?"

What I learned that day—and several times since—was that when a child asks a question, the first thing we need to ask ourselves is, what is she really asking? Is the question actually simpler than it seems? Does she want a logical answer, or is she really looking for reassurance? What does she *really* want to know?

How can I respond in a way that will help my child grow? Spiritually nurturing responses to difficult questions address the child's everyday experience, using a minimum of pious language. In fact, when we speak in overly "religious" terms, we run the risk of cutting off conversation. "Why do frogs have eyes on top of their heads?" asked Matthew one morning as I drove him and Laura to day camp at the nature center.

"Because," I answered, not yet fully awake, "that's the way God made them."

There was silence in the backseat. Then Laura, who was almost four at the time, had an idea. "Tonight, when I pray to God, I think I'm going to ask him *why* he made them that way," she said. "And Mom, if you pray, too, why don't *you* ask him?"

Out of the mouths of babes, I thought, and decided to try for a recovery: "Let's pretend we're frogs sitting on lily pads with eyes on top of our heads, and see what we can see." In the rearview mirror I saw them put their index fingers on their heads, and as we imagined life from a frog's perspective, I sensed that they were learning something about the wonder of creation in a way that felt right—without any pious words from me.

Something More...

. . .

*E*ncouraging our child's questioning is often challenging during the early childhood years, because he tends to cling to "answers" of his own. "Where does God live?" asked a three-year-old, who then answered her own question. "*I* know—up in the sky. God is the sun, his wife is the sunset, and Jesus is their child. They gave him to Mary."

As we saw in chapter 5, the preschooler's thinking reflects his rich fantasy life. Not surprisingly, it is important to guard against the tendency to chuckle at his theology, or to rush in and correct him. A simple, "I'm glad you told me that," or "It's interesting to wonder what God is like, isn't it?" will keep the door open to future discussion. And we can continue providing our child with stories that help broaden his perspective. A simple poem that speaks of God in terms of the love in our hearts, or a Native American legend of Mother Earth, can help bring God closer in the child's mind. (*See appendix.*)

As the child reaches six or seven and his thinking becomes more concrete, his interpretations take a literal turn. If a child asks, "Who wrote the Bible?" for example, and the answer is "God," he is most likely to imagine a bearded, grandfatherly figure sitting down at a table, pen in hand. Instead we can offer a simple reply which he is less likely to distort. "I told my son the Bible was a lot of books put together, each one written by people who felt very close to God," said one mother of a seven-year-old.

"Who is God?" asked one six-year-old boy.

"In the desert he told Moses, 'I am who I am,'" said his mother, a college teacher. "He didn't say exactly who he is, because you can't put God in a box."

"Yeah, God is a *lot* bigger than a box," replied the boy.

..."Why Does God Make Bad People?"

This mother had recognized that the "definitions" of God many of us heard as children—of an "all-powerful, all-knowing" being—tend to reduce the divine to a kind of invisible superhero. But her use of metaphor had confused her child. Fortunately, there are ways of sharing our sense of God's wonder in terms that make sense to our children. With a school-age child—and indeed, with *any* age group—we can communicate more effectively by keeping our explanations *close to his concrete experience*. If a child of this age asks, "Who is God?" we can begin by encouraging him to share his own impressions. What has he learned about God? Does he ever feel especially close to God?

Now we can share one or two of our own experiences of "who God is." Rather than offering a list of adjectives, we can help our child learn about the character of God by recognizing what God *does*. God gave Mommy and Daddy two beautiful children, for example. God made the apple blossoms bloom in the backyard yesterday. God put love in people's hearts so our town decided to start a food pantry. We may also wish to draw on stories from our tradition. God brought the people of Israel to the land of milk and honey. By encouraging a child to draw his own conclusions about God's character rather than handing him abstract descriptions, we offer opportunities for real growth.

How do I speak in terms my child will understand?
Choosing developmentally appropriate *language* to explain every concept is often not possible, especially with young children, because many religious concepts are simply beyond their grasp. (Those of us who grew up memorizing simplistic definitions of sophisticated theological ideas know only too well how hard it is, later on, to breathe new life into them.) What we *can* do is affirm and enlarge our children's glimmerings of understanding through their own experience.

Something More...

> *One should lie empty, open, choiceless as a beach—waiting for a gift from the sea.*
>
> —Anne Morrow Lindbergh

With young children, we need to speak in terms of the world they can see and touch. This is not always as simple as it sounds.

Seven-year-old Kathy asked her mother, "How can we help poor people?"

By way of an answer, Kathy's mother suggested that she choose a few outgrown toys in good condition to donate to children at a local shelter for homeless families. They packed up cartons of dolls, musical instruments, and interlocking plastic blocks, and drove down to the shelter.

Mother and daughter brought them into the shelter office, shared by a social worker and a secretary, but Kathy never saw any of the shelter's residents. Later, as they were fastening their seat belts for the trip home, Kathy let out a whoop. "Boy, the people who live there are a lot richer than *we* are," she said. "They even have *secretaries* and lots of typewriters!"

Kathy's "conclusion" was perfectly logical, of course, from the point of view of a six- or seven-year-old. Kathy's mother had realized that her daughter needed a concrete, hands-on response. If Kathy had actually had the opportunity to present the toys in person to the children at the shelter, the experience would have been even more meaningful to her. This might have best happened as an outgrowth of a *relationship* with one or two of the children developed over time—through outings to the park, for example, at school, at an arts-and-crafts program at the library, or after a few playtime visits to the shelter. As children get to know one another on an informal basis, we begin to notice that instead of talking about "poor people" they are mentioning friends by name.

When the child is as young as five, speaking in terms he can understand is a real challenge, because his limited concept of *fairness* (which is roughly equivalent to "getting the same treatment as everybody else") takes precedence in his mind over spiritual values such as love and sharing. "Why should *I* have to help clean up," one boy asked his mother indignantly after a barbecue, "when all the other people left without doing anything?" Although the child begins to outgrow this tit-for-tat morality by nine or ten, when he learns to see things more readily from another's point of view, even at this age God may be understood as the equivalent of a "conscience," administering punishment to wrongdoers with more justice than mercy. As the child grows beyond concrete operational thought, he will begin to reflect on the reality of injustice in the world, on his own lack of perfection, and on the conflicts and discrepancies in many of his previous ideas. His skeptical questions and comments will reflect a readiness for a more complex, personal spirituality.

In the next section we shall explore many of the most frequent questions children ask at different ages, and hear answers from some thoughtful parents. There is no single moment when we "deliver enlightenment" to our child, or when we feel any more certain than Pooh that we've caught up with the answer we're tracking. When logical answers elude us, sometimes a hug can express a world of empathy and hope. And as we open our hearts and minds to the possibilities, and consider what we can learn by exploring our traditions, we begin to help our child grow toward God's own answers.

*   *   *

And I think—but I am not sure—that that is why he was always called Pooh.

"Why did Sally's grandma die?" "Did God really make me?" "Why doesn't God stop cars from crashing?" Children's questions cover a range of material that would humble the average seminary student. For the most part they can be grouped into several key categories, each more perplexing than the next: death, the nature of God, the origins of life, the meaning of suffering, and the beliefs of others. We'll consider each category and learn how a number of parents have dealt with these questions. Usually, as we shall see, the most helpful response is not an easy answer, but the one that enables our child's ongoing process of exploration.

Obviously, there is more to answering hard questions than simply finding developmentally appropriate answers. Every parent's response reflects a combination of personal experience, religious background, and an intimate, God-given relationship with our child that can guide us more surely than any book. For this reason, it may be helpful to take a few moments to focus on your own thoughts and experiences. You may wish to jot down some notes on a sheet of paper or in your journal. As you read the questions that follow, ask yourself:

• What is your immediate emotional response to the question?
• Has your child asked a question of this type?

..."Why Does God Make Bad People?"

- Looking back on your own life experience, can you think of an event or relationship that has in some way contributed to your understanding of this issue? Could you share it with your child?
- Based on the teachings you have received in church or synagogue, and perhaps on your own reading, does your faith tradition seem to be a resource that can help you respond to the question? How has it *not* been helpful?
- How might you answer your child if he asked you the same question today?

Who made the world? Who made me? Did God really make my sister? When a young child asks questions about the origins of life, many parents worry that mentioning God is somehow trapping her in a primitive view of the world literally based on the Genesis myth. "*I* certainly believe in evolution, and I wouldn't want my kid to think it all started with Adam and Eve," said one father.

Our creation stories do not tell us literally how the world began, of course. Instead, like a first snapshot taken of mother and newborn baby, they are handed down to us as reminders of our bright beginnings. We convey this to our children in different ways at each stage of life.

With a toddler or preschooler, we can emphasize that God made the world and said it was good; that God loves it just the way Mommy and Daddy love their child.

Six- and seven-year-olds often insist on knowing the mechanics of the process. They are aware that God doesn't actually *make* the babies, the way candy is made in a factory, and they may be very interested in eggs and sperm. Now the beauty and wonder of God's ongoing creation process can be shared through observation of everyday natural events—the birth of a litter of kittens, for example, or life in an anthill. "Each time a new baby is born, or a new leaf grows on a tree, God is bringing a wonderful new life into the world," one mother told her second-grader.

As the child grows older, he may be fascinated to learn about the diversity of animal and plant life around the globe, as well as the process of evolution. At this point in his life, science and spirit may appear to be opposing forces. He will find nurture in opportunities to integrate his increasingly sophisticated grasp of scientific concepts and his spiritual awareness. Books or opportunities to discuss creation-centered spirituality (as distinguished from creationist theology) may be helpful. (*See Resources for Further Exploration in the appendix.*)

What happens to us after we die? Questions about death and the afterlife often come up when a child finds a dead bird in the backyard, or when a pet dies. Although most of us feel uncomfortable talking about death and are saddened by the thought of discussing it with our children ("It broke my heart to hear my sweet little three-year-old talking about his dead grandpa," said one mother), they are often more willing than we think to face the subject openly.

When a *three-year-old* asks about death, it is helpful to keep in mind that he does not really understand it as permanent or irreversible. For him it tends to amount to a long sleep—like Snow White's time in the glass casket—and reincarnation is an idea that seems to come naturally. By the age of four, however, fear of death is common. "Why did Nana die?" one four-year-old asked his mother repeatedly after her mother-in-law's sudden death. At this stage a simple but *reassuring* answer is most helpful: "She died because she had a long happy life and she got very old."

...."Why Does God Make Bad People?"

If you feel comfortable talking about life after death, don't be surprised if your child assumes that Nana is up in heaven with his pet goldfish and the neighbors' old dog.

With a *six- or seven-year-old,* we can respond to questions about death in terms appropriate to his concrete thinking by providing opportunities to look upon death as a part of life. He can encounter change and death in the natural world: caterpillars turning into butterflies, tadpoles becoming frogs, leaves falling from trees.

At this age questions about death tend to catapult us faster than we'd like into the afterlife—or at least into detailed descriptions thereof. Where do people go when they die? What is heaven? Will you love me after you're dead? Can Grandpa see us? Do people drive cars in heaven? "When my mother died I talked about heaven with my daughter because I thought that was the easiest way to discuss death, even though I'm not sure about heaven myself," said the mother of a six-year-old. "But when she starts asking for details, I'm at a loss."

A child's concept of heaven has a Disney quality at this point, and he demands an often-baffling level of detail. It helps to keep this in mind, especially if we are less than confident about our own understanding of—or belief in—an afterlife.

"Will our family be together after we die?" asked a five-year-old boy.

"I'm not sure," said his mother. "Some people think we'll see everybody we love. Other people say we'll feel very close to everybody in the world. Anyway, I think we'll feel very peaceful." Another mother, knowing her child was fascinated by science, told him about near-death experiences, the reports by large numbers of critically ill people who have described encounters with a bright light and a feeling of peace.

And one mother told her seven-year-old, after the death of

his grandmother, that her spirit had passed into another world. But as children reach school age and begin asking for details, we can be most helpful by avoiding descriptions of heaven that make it sound like a place that can be located geographically, a sort of "happy hunting ground."

We can best describe the afterlife in terms of life in the here and now. "The different life after we die isn't going to be flying out in space among the stars," one mother told her worried six-year-old. "It's going to be like getting a big hug from your Mom." In this way, she drew on her child's concrete experience to suggest that heaven is not a place, but a state of love and joy.

The *ten- or eleven-year-old* will be ready for a new level of questioning. He learns about tragic deaths in the news—victims of natural disasters such as earthquakes and hurricanes—and may know what it means to lose a school friend to a terminal illness, or to an intoxicated driver. How can God let these things happen? he wonders. At this point, the child needs to be able to express bewilderment and anger at home and in the company of other thoughtful, caring adults. No child should be subjected to platitudes (e.g., "It's God's will") that discount his emotional responses. Love and the affirmation of life are the hallmarks of our Western religious traditions, and we convey them not by insisting that our child look on the "bright side," but through our patient and nonjudgmental willingness to share his pain. Hope also grows through personal involvement. Encouraging our child to learn about organizations such as the Red Cross, candy stripers, and Students Against Drunk Driving (SADD) is a way to help him discover how, even in the midst of tragedy, God works among us and picks up the pieces.

Few of us would willingly introduce our children to the concept of hell. Threats of the devil or hell should *never* be used as a disciplinary measure, either at home or in Sunday school. When children are subjected to such intimidation, it strikes at their deepest fears and only undermines the sense of loving connectedness that is the goal of spiritual nurture. Are the bad things I do, and the mean thoughts I have about my brother, so terrible that I'm going to end up *really* in trouble? Is God someone who punishes? Children, unless they are victims of abuse, have enormous difficulty comprehending contradictory images of God; love and cruelty do not go together.

Who is God? As we saw in chapter 6, three-year-olds approach the concepts of God and the spirit in highly imaginative ways. More often than not, when a preschooler asks a question about the nature of God, he can be encouraged to answer it for himself. "God is the sky," said one small boy happily, and he left it at that. At this age a child can accept an explanation that might seem vague to a school-age child: "God makes us alive," for example, or "God is love."

Six- and seven-year-olds, however, are eager for more specific details. Where does God live? Can I see God? Is my spirit in my stomach? With the encouragement of television shows featuring ghosts, children understand the relationship between spirit and body, and between God and humanity, in highly dualistic ways. God is a "spirit" who lives up in heaven on a cloud. "Spirit" is something *attached* to a person's body, like Superman's cape.

We can help prevent confusing our child further by understanding for ourselves that "spirit" refers not to a separate, "holy" appendage, but to the *whole person* who is in relationship with God and creation. Keeping this in mind, rather than offering elaborate "descriptions" of God or the spirit, we can encourage our child to recognize and share experiences of God's

203

love in his heart and active presence in his everyday life. "You can see *some* parts of yourself with your eyes—like your arms and legs," one mother told her five-year-old. "There are other parts of you—like the way you love your baby sister—you can't see with your eyes. But they're still part of you. And all of you is your spirit."

I asked some first-graders if they had noticed times when they really felt God being with them, for example. Their answers showed surprising insights. "When my Mommy hugs me," said one child. "When I see my baby brother sleeping," said another. And another felt God's presence "when I help set the table."

Older children can be encouraged to share their own experiences of the presence of God, and their understanding of the character of God. As they begin to struggle with the reality of human pain, they are often ready to explore the idea (common to both the Jewish and Christian traditions) that God is present and active even in the midst of suffering.

What about people of other religions? Why don't we go to Tim's church? How come we don't have a menorah (or a Christmas tree)? Why is that man wearing that weird hat? A child learns religious tolerance less from our "enlightened" answers than from our own day-to-day attitude toward people of other faith traditions.

With preschoolers, we convey our respect for different ways of observance by giving our children opportunities to share them. Three-year-olds are eager to try the foods and rituals their preschool friends enjoy in their homes. Around a holiday, ask a friend to introduce you and your child to some traditional dishes and customs.

Six- and seven-year-olds enjoy hearing the stories associated with the different holidays. They are very interested in exploring the perspectives of others and are ready to learn how people of other traditions mark weddings, births, and deaths. (*For information on other faith traditions, see Resources for Further Exploration.*) When they ask questions about people of other faiths, we need not pretend that all religions are alike. Instead we can reassure them that God, who made all different kinds of people who know him in many different ways, loves us all.

"We don't have a menorah because we're not Jewish," I told my children simply when they asked one December. They had made construction-paper menorahs in school. "Jewish people light the candles on the menorah to remember something very special that happened a long time ago." I told them the story of Chanukah, of the lamp that miraculously burned for eight days, and of Judah Maccabee's fight for religious freedom. And since every December in our home we light the candles on an Advent wreath, we talked about how candles help people of many different religions feel close to God.

"If we had been alive during that story, we would have decided to be Jewish, wouldn't we, Mom?" asked one of the children. For the first time, he had seen beyond the "missing" Christmas trees in the homes of his Jewish friends, and beyond the much-envied eight whole days of presents. In time he will learn that religious traditions are not picked up or put down quite so easily. But for now, he seemed to be getting the point.

With older children, questions arise about religious prejudice and hatred. Why did someone write anti-Semitic words on the wall of the synagogue last night? Why did so many people cooperate with Hitler? Why do countries fight religious wars? As always, they need to be able to share their feelings with caring adults. In a youth group setting or at home, they may wish to discuss such painful subjects as the Holocaust, and the battles raging in Northern Ireland, and the crisis in the Middle

East. Children can only trust us when we truthfully acknowledge the realities of prejudice and violence and their tragic consequences, rather than attempt to gloss over them. Only then do our stories of the selfless efforts of ordinary people—in the World War II underground, for example, and the peace movements of our time—help them grapple with religious hatred without despair.

Why isn't life fair? A child will not put the question in such a general way, of course. Instead, he will ask, Why don't some people have homes? Why are some children troublemakers in school? Why do people die in earthquakes? Why do others die of AIDS?

Our children's questions about pain and suffering must be the hardest ones of all. We lack explanations. We wish we could offer them a happier world, or one that made more sense.

And we wish children did not take so readily to the idea that all misfortune is punishment for bad behavior. "Mommy, why is that man poor?" asked one four-year-old who saw a homeless man walking along the street.

"He probably doesn't have a job, or he doesn't make enough money to pay for a place to live," said his mother.

"Why, was he *bad*?" asked the child.

As we have discussed, this child was reflecting a moral viewpoint typical of preschoolers and school-age children, who believe that just as doing the right thing brings rewards, a person who has *not* been rewarded must have done the wrong thing. (Many adults, of course, have similar attitudes toward welfare recipients and people with AIDS.) Unfortunately, this point of view is reinforced when the child hears fairy tales that depict rich people as good and kind, and poor people or hunchbacks as mean or bad. We can help him grow by choosing books by contemporary authors that present poor or disabled people as flesh-and-blood human beings with much to share.

When a young child asks a question about pain or innocent suffering, we need to remember that he is not looking for an abstract explanation, but wanting to know whether he himself is safe from harm, and whether the world is a place he can trust. Do hurricanes knock down houses in *our* town? Will a burglar break into *our* house? Will a kidnapper get *me?*

Although we may not be able to offer unqualified reassurance, we can give answers that are honest but hopeful and convey a sense of empowerment and trust in God's sustaining care in the face of evil. "Well, Mommy and Daddy and your teacher are taking good care of you, and you're beginning to learn how to take care of yourself a little, now that you know about stranger danger." "Nobody used to worry at all about toxic waste when I was a child, and it's a very big problem, but now lots of people are using their brains to figure out how to work on it."

As the child approaches seven or eight and learns to think from the perspectives of others, we can help him cope with his questions by joining with others who are exploring their own connections with suffering people, who are choosing to participate in God's life-giving action. We can help bag groceries at a food pantry, write a letter to a member of Congress, volunteer at a hospital, correspond with a Native American child.

An older child's questions about pain and suffering often point to the gap between the values he has learned and the reality he is encountering in our world. Although we may find his concerns about injustice, violence, and pollution overwhelming, and we may be tempted to tell him he is "too idealistic," we need not attempt to paint a rosier picture. Ironically, pretending that sweetness and light are the only reality ultimately leads to despair. "The teenage kids of sixties' 'flower children' are incredibly cynical," remarked a clerical friend of mine who has worked for years with youth groups. "To them, peace and love don't seem to have anything to do with real life." An adolescent will respond to shared stories and experiences that *affirm* his painful perceptions and only then offer hope. (The story of Ryan White, the boy who contracted AIDS and helped raise awareness about AIDS among children and adults across the country, is an obvious example of God's working in the midst of pain.) With time and understanding, we and other caring, involved adults and peers can help our child grow toward an awareness that good can come out of suffering. We do not understand why evil and suffering exist in the world. But we can help our child recognize that somehow humanity is given the strength and wisdom to survive, and even to move forward.

10. *The Road Ahead*

Once there was a little bunny who wanted to run away. So he said to his mother, "I am running away."

"If you run away," said his mother, "I will run after you.

For you are my little bunny."

—*THE RUNAWAY BUNNY*,
MARGARET WISE BROWN

Labor Day. Our little girl will start nursery school in just a few days, and her brother will be riding off on a big yellow school bus to kindergarten. This morning we are spreading out a picnic blanket in the backyard. Canada geese waddle past us on the grass, and dragonflies hover over the pond. As I unpack a basket of sandwiches, the kids chase each other around a stand of birches. Sunlight on their hair, cotton shorts baggy over skinny legs, flip-flops on their soft feet: how lovely, how full of life they are.

Something More...

But their childish voices float across the yard. "After kindergarten comes first grade," I hear one child call out.

"Second grade, third grade, fourth grade," his sister chimes in. "Fifth grade, sixth grade, seventh grade." The chant goes on and on, pounding into my heart, up to twelfth grade.

"And *then* we'll go to college," her brother concludes triumphantly, "and you'll *never* see us!"

Seeing my sudden tears, they run over and wrap their arms around my neck. Their skin is sticky, and their T-shirts smell slightly sour in the summer heat. "You'll *always* be our mommy," they promise solemnly.

The boy kneels in the grass and looks deep into my eyes. "Even after you're *dead* you'll be our mommy, and we'll bring flowers and visit your tombstone every day," he adds.

I once read a Buddhist meditation that advised seekers of enlightenment to "act as if their turbans were ablaze, for death is surely bound to come." As parents, we get daily reminders from our unsuspecting children that our own turbans are on fire. Usually they come in the form of the little changes we notice. A pair of jeans, too long a few months ago, end up as hand-me-downs. The first tooth falls out (Didn't it just come in?) and goes under a pillow for the tooth fairy. Our children demand so much attention for the first few hectic years. Yet before we know it they want, like the bunny in Margaret Wise Brown's story, to run away.

They are flesh of our flesh, more precious than we ever dreamed, but they are not ours. They need to explore on their own, to learn for themselves, even when it brings them pain— even when it brings *us* pain. We all know this, and day by day we live in the tension between loving and letting go. "Being a parent teaches you what selfless giving really means," one father told me ruefully.

Your children are not your children.
They are the sons and daughters of Life's longing for
    itself.
They come through you but not from you,
And though they are with you yet they belong not to
    you.
You may give them your love but not your thoughts,
For they have their own thoughts.
You may house their bodies but not their souls,
For their souls dwell in the house of tomorrow, which
    you cannot visit, not even in your dreams.
You may strive to be like them, but seek not to make
    them like you.
For life goes not backward nor tarries with yesterday.
                    —*Kahlil Gibran,* The Prophet *(1923)*

"If you become a crocus in a hidden
garden," said his mother, "I will be a
gardener. And I will find you."

One of our most ancient lessons about spiritual nurture is the biblical story of Samuel and Eli. Samuel is a young boy who lives in the temple. Clothed in a ceremonial ephod, or apron, he is "growing in the presence of the Lord." Eli is Samuel's spiritual guide, a priest of the temple who is going blind in his old age.

One night Eli is sleeping near the ark of the convenant, and

Samuel is lying nearby. In the darkness the Lord calls Samuel's name. But the boy, thinking he is hearing Eli's voice, runs to the old priest to wake him up. Eli, bewildered, tells Samuel to go back to sleep.

But the Lord calls out to Samuel again, and once more the child awakens Eli, only to be sent away.

Finally, when the Lord calls Samuel for the third time, Eli realizes what is going on. Samuel has outgrown his teacher. Now the child is hearing the voice of God directly, in his own heart. "Go, lie down," Eli tells his young charge; "and if he calls you, you shall say, 'Speak, LORD, for thy servant hears.' "

As parents and spiritual nurturers, we often, like Eli, need to be reawakened to our real task. Ours is not to mold our child according to our own vision, but to help her become the person she was born to be. We need to ask ourselves not "How can I tell this child about God or the life of the spirit?" but instead, "What is God doing in this child?" and "Who is she in the process of becoming?"

As we begin to consider this question, we discover that a kind of love we might never have known ourselves capable of— a *self-giving* love—is taking root and growing within our hearts. "My child is the first person I've ever known, beyond all doubts, for whom I'd run without thinking in front of a speeding car," said one father. As our own spirituality deepens, we gain perspective and wisdom that sustain us in our lives as parents. "What I didn't realize before I discovered this faith in God for myself," reflected one mother of an infant and a six-year-old, "was how much effect it would have on my day-to-day anxiety about mothering. But it does. I worry less about my effectiveness in little problems, and instead I'm looking at the long term. I'm understanding that my children's lives have an underlying spiritual purpose."

. . . The Road Ahead

And we grow to understand that our own lives have a spiritual purpose, too—that the incredible love for our child teaches us a new way of relating to the world. As we draw strength from the nurturing connection with our own child, many parents grow increasingly aware that for many other children of the next generation, these bonds of love and care have broken down. In the midst of the crowded days of young parenting, many of the men and women I have spoken to are seeking to reach out to children and adults who are less fortunate, and to care for the earth which we are passing on. It is a time of awakening.

We cannot accompany our child all along her spiritual journey. But as we prepare for the day she overtakes us, we can help her find her true direction. And, with slow and often hesitating steps, we can make our own way along the road ahead.

Appendix

"Hanging over our roof
there is a star as a window . . ."

—*AMAHL AND THE NIGHT VISITORS*,
GIAN CARLO MENOTTI

It is not often easy to offer our children logical explanations of spiritual questions, but we can always tell them a story. Stories and songs find a place in the heart and speak directly to the child's spirit.

In simple, down-to-earth language, stories open our eyes to the world we live in and to the wisdom of our collective past. They offer visions of worlds full of challenges and adventures that mirror the conflicts and crises our children face every day. As we curl up on a sofa or bed with our child for the

215

intimacy of story time, we reach out to all of life. Through stories, every child can share the wonder of Gian Carlo Menotti's Amahl, who looks up at the sky and sees the Star of Bethlehem as "a star as large as a window."

Folk and fairy tales and stories from other lands, Native American legends and Greek myths: by sharing these traditional narratives with our children, we help them dip into the spiritual riches of generations of people all over the world. What is truly important in life? What is courage? Can people triumph over evil? These and other questions have been the stuff of traditional stories for millennia.

BOOKS

As you will see, the books on the listing that follows are a diverse group. They reflect many cultures and traditions; they appeal to various age groups (as indicated) and temperaments. What they all have in common is a way of capturing our imagination and opening our eyes to the wonders all around us. They are available in libraries, bookstores, and by mail from the catalogues listed in Resources for Further Exploration (appendix).

If you would like to share **Native American** stories, try: Gretchen Will Mayo's illustrated *Earthmaker's Tales* or *Star Tales* (Walker and Company, 1989); *The Girl Who Loved Wild Horses*, written and illustrated by Paul Goble (Bradbury Press, 1978); *Keepers of the Earth*, by Michael J. Caduto and Joseph Bruchac, with stories and hands-on activities (Fulcrum, 1989); and *The Legend of Scarface*, by Robert San Souci.

For legends and tales from **Asian** cultures, look for *The Mountains of Tibet*, written and illustrated by Mordicai Gerstein (Harper and Row, 1987); *Seasons of Splendor*, a collection of Indian

. . . Appendix

myths and legends arranged by holiday and season by Madhur Jaffrey, illustrated by Michael Foreman (Puffin, 1985); and *Animalia*, a collection of stories about the saints, books of Chinese tales, and the story of the Buddha's life, written and illustrated by Barbara Berger (Celestial Arts, 1982).

Among the **African** folk tales you and your child will enjoy sharing are *Bringing the Rain to Kapiti Plain*, written by Verna Aardema and illustrated by Beatriz Vidal (Dial, 1981); *Mufaro's Beautiful Daughters: An African Tale*, written and illustrated by John Steptoe (Mulberg, 1987); and *Why Mosquitoes Buzz in People's Ears: A West African Tale*, written by Verna Aardema and illustrated by Leo and Diane Dillon (Dial, 1975). Also recommended is *The People Could Fly: American Black Folktales*, by Virginia Hamilton, illustrated Leo and Diane Dillon (Knopf, 1985).

There is a wide range of retellings of traditional **European** folk tales available, from many different cultures: *Babushka: An Old Russian Folktale*, written and illustrated by Charles Mikolaycak (Holiday, 1984); *Zlateh the Goat and Other Stories*, by Isaac Bashevis Singer (Harper and Row, 1966); *It Could Always Be Worse: A Yiddish Folk Tale*, written and illustrated by Margot Zemach (Scholastic, 1987); *Saint George and the Dragon*, retold by Margaret Hodges and illustrated by Trina Schart Hyman (Little, Brown, 1984); *Sir Gawain and the Loathly Lady*, retold by Selina Hastings and illustrated by Juan Wijngaard (Lothrop, Lee & Shepard, 1985); *Daniel O'Rourke*, a classic Irish tale written and illustrated by Gerald McDermott (Puffin, 1986); and *The Boy Who Held Back the Sea*, retold by Lenny Hort, illustrated by Thomas Locker (Dial Books, 1988).

For **Greek and Roman myths,** look for *A Child's Book of Myths and Enchantment Tales*, by Margaret Price Evans (Macmillan, 1986); the classic *D'Aulaire's Book of Greek Myths* (Doubleday, 1962); *The Macmillan Book of Greek Gods and Heroes*, by Alice Low and illustrated by Arvis Stewart (Macmillan, 1985); and *Classic Myths to Read Aloud*, William F. Russell, ed. (Crown, 1984). Older children enjoy *The Children's Homer: The Adventures of Odysseus and the Tale of Troy*, written by Padraic Colum and illustrated by Willy Pogany (Macmillan, 1918).

Two other collections to look for are *The Maid of the North: Feminist Folk Tales from Around the World*, by Ethel Johnston Phelps, illustrated by Lloyd Bloom (Holt, 1981), and *Beginnings: Creation Myths of the World* by Penelope Farmer.

A **fairy tale,** Bruno Bettelheim observed, is like a "a deep, quiet pool which at first seems to reflect only our own image, but behind it we discover the inner turmoils of our soul—its depths, and ways to gain peace within ourselves and with the world." There are many beautifully illustrated retellings available, among them *The Ugly Duckling*, by Hans Christian Andersen, retold by Marianna Mayer and illustrated by Thomas Locker (Macmillan, 1987); *The Nightingale*, by Hans Christian Andersen, illustrated by Nancy Ekholm Burkert (Harper and Row, 1965); *The Sleeping Beauty*, retold and illustrated by Trina Schart Hyman (Little, Brown, 1977); *Sleeping Beauty* (Macmillan, 1984) and *Beauty and the Beast* (Aladdin, 1979), both retold and illustrated by Mercer Mayer; *The Snow Queen*, by Hans Christian Andersen, translated by Naomi Lewis and illustrated by Angela Barrett (Henry Holt, 1988); *Snow White and the Seven Dwarfs*, retold by Randall Jarrell and illustrated by Nancy Ekholm Burkert (Farrar, Straus and Giroux, 1972); *The Wild Swans*, by Hans Christian Andersen, illustrated by Susan Jeffers (Dial, 1981); *The Ugly Duckling*, by Hans Christian Andersen, illustrated by Robert Van Nutt (Knopf, 1986); *Tomie de Paola's Favorite Nursery Tales* (Putnam, 1986); and *Ardizzone's Hans Andersen: Fourteen Classic Tales*, illustrated by Edward Ardizzone (Deutsch, 1985).

... Appendix

Books of **poetry** help us and our children see everyday life in fresh new ways: choose an appealing version of *A Child's Garden of Verse*, by Robert Louis Stevenson; read *Hiawatha* by Henry Wadsworth Longfellow, illustrated by Susan Jeffers (Dial Books for Young Readers, 1983); *Stopping by Woods on a Snowy Evening*, by Robert Frost, illustrated by Susan Jeffers (E. P. Dutton, 1978); *The Random House Book of Poetry for Children*, Jack Prelutsky, ed., illustrated by Arnold Lobel (Random House, 1983); and *Read-Aloud Rhymes for the Very Young*, selected by Jack Prelutsky, illustrated by Marc Brown (Knopf, 1986).

There is an abundance of children's books to help children in their explorations of **community:** Where do I fit in? How are other people like me? How are they different? Who was here before me? Books that offer touching insights into family life include *Love You Forever*, by Robert Munsch (Firefly Books, Ltd., 1982); Charlotte Zolotow's *The Summer Night* (1971) and *A Father Like That* (1974) (Harper and Row); *The Runaway Bunny*, by Margaret Wise Brown, illustrated by Clement Hurd (Harper and Row, 1942); *Goldie the Dollmaker*, by M. B. Goffstein (Farrar, Straus and Giroux, 1969); *The Velveteen Rabbit*, by Margery Williams, illustrated by William Nicholson (Avon, 1922, and now in many editions); *Where the Wild Things Are*, written and illustrated by Maurice Sendak (Harper and Row, 1963); *Corduroy*, by Don Freeman (Puffin, 1968), and *A Pocket for Corduroy; Bedtime Hugs for Little Ones* by Debby Boone, illustrated Gabriel Ferrer (Harvest House, 1988); *Grandma and Grandpa*, by Helen Oxenbury (Dial, 1984); *Even If I Did Something Awful*, by Barbara Shook Hazen, illustrated by Nancy Kincade (Atheneum, 1981); *Daddy Doesn't Live Here Anymore*, by Betty Boegehold, illustrated by Deborah Borgo (Golden, 1985); *Alexander and the Terrible, Horrible, No Good, Very Bad Day*, by Judith Viorst, illustrated by Ray Cruz (Atheneum, 1972); *Charlotte's Web*, by E. B. White (Harper and

Appendix . . .

Row, 1952); all the Ramona books by Beverly Cleary—*Ramona the Brave*, *Ramona the Pest*, *Ramona Forever*, etc. (Dell); *The Two of Them*, by Aliki (Greenwillow, 1979); *A Wrinkle in Time*, by Madeleine L'Engle (Farrar, Straus and Giroux, 1962); *A Baby Sister for Frances*, by Russell Hoban, illustrated by Lillian Hoban (Harper and Row, 1964); *Knots on a Counting Rope*, by Bill Martin, Jr., and John Archambault, illustrated by Ted Rand (Henry Holt, 1987); *101 Things to Do with a Baby*, by Jan Ormerod (Lothrop, 1984); *Something on My Mind*, written by Nikki Grimes, illustrated by Tom Feelings (Dial, 1978); *The Patchwork Quilt*, by Verley Flournoy, illustrated by Jerry Pinkney (Dial, 1985); *Annie and the Old One*, by Miska Miles, illustrated by Peter Parnall (Little, Brown, 1971); *The Tenth Good Thing About Barney*, written by Judith Viorst, illustrated by Eric Blegvad (Aladdin, 1971); *The Story About Ping*, by Marjorie Flack (Penguin, 1977); *Frog and Toad Are Friends*, by Arnold Lobel (Harper and Row, 1970); *Moonlight*, written and illustrated by Jan Ormerod (Puffin, 1982), and also *Sunshine; Amos & Boris*, written and illustrated by William Steig (Penguin, 1971); and, for middle readers, *Stories for Children* (Farrar, Straus and Giroux, 1984). To begin your own family history, look for *My Book About Me*, by Dr. Seuss and Roy McKie (Random House, 1969) and *Mom Remembers: A Treasury of Memories for My Child* (Harper and Row, 1990).

Books that help broaden a child's perspective and increase awareness of the **diversity** of our global community include *People*, by Peter Spier (Doubleday, 1980); *Why Does That Man Have Such a Big Nose?* by Mary Beth Quinsey (Parenting Press, 1986); *The Story of Ferdinand*, by Munro Leaf, illustrated by Robert Lawson (Viking, 1977); *Abiyoyo*, written by Pete Seeger, illustrated by Michael Hays (Macmillan, 1986); *The Way to Start a Day*, by Byrd Baylor, illustrated by Peter Parnall (Aladdin, 1978); *Anno's Counting Book*, written and illustrated by Mitsumasa Anno

(Harper and Row, 1977); *Anno's Journey*, written and illustrated by Mitsumasa Anno (Philomel, 1978), and also *Anno's Britain*, *Anno's Italy*, and *Anno's Medieval World*; *A Day on the Avenue*, written and illustrated by Robert Roennfelt (Viking, 1984); *Jerusalem, Shining Still*, by Karla Kuskin, woodcuts by David Frampton (Harper and Row, 1987); *The Three Astronauts*, by Umberto Eco and Eugenio Carmi (Harcourt Brace Jovanovich, 1989); and, for older readers and listeners, *Watership Down*, by Richard Adams (Avon, 1974). Some of the most notable books on **the journey of life** for older readers include *Are You There, God—It's Me, Margaret*, by Judy Blume (Bradbury, 1970); *Bridge to Terabithia*, by Katherine Paterson (Crowell, 1977); *Island of the Blue Dolphins*, by Scott O'Dell (Houghton Mifflin, 1960); *The Lion, the Witch, and the Wardrobe*, by C. S. Lewis (Macmillan, 1951); and *Julie of the Wolves*, by Jean Craighead George (Harper and Row, 1973), and also *My Side of the Mountain* (Dutton, 1959).

For stories that invite children into communities of **history,** look for *My Backyard History Book*, by David Weitzman (Little, Brown, 1975); *How Many Days to America*, by Eve Buntin, illustrated by Beth Peck (Clarion Books, 1988); *All-of-a-Kind Family*, about life for a Jewish family on New York's Lower East Side, by Sydney Taylor, illustrated Helen John (Yearling, 1951); *Squanto and the First Thanksgiving*, by Joyce K. Kessel (Carolrhoda Books, 1986); *Sam the Minuteman*, by Nathaniel Benchley, illustrated by Arnold Lobel (Harper and Row, 1969); *Johnny Tremain*, by Esther Forbes (Dell, 1943); *Caddie Woodlawn*, by Carol Ryrie Brink (Macmillan, 1935); *A Day No Pigs Would Die*, by Robert Newton Peck (Knopf, 1972); *If You Sailed on the Mayflower, If You Lived with the Sioux Indians, Wanted Dead or Alive: The True Story of Harriet Tubman*, all by Ann McGovern (Scholastic, 1969); The Little House books by Laura Ingalls Wilder (*Little House in*

Appendix . . .

the Big Woods, and so on, Harper, 1932); *The Pilgrims of Plimoth*, written and illustrated by Marcia Sewall (Atheneum, 1986); the Barron's "Journey Through History" series for young children, including *Prehistory to Egypt, The Greek and Roman Eras, The Middle Ages, The Renaissance, Modern Times*, and *The Contemporary Age* (Barron's Educational Series, 1988); and, for older readers, *The Landmark History of the American People*, by Daniel J. Boorstin (Random House, 1987). Other titles appropriate only for *older* children—and you may wish to consider reading these aloud, or at least making time to talk them over after your child reads them—include *My Hiroshima* (for older readers and listeners), by Junko Morimoto (Viking, 1987); *The Night Journey*, about a Jewish family's escape from Russian pogroms, by Kathryn Lasky, with drawings by Trina Schart Hyman (Warner, 1982); *The Upstairs Room*, by Johanna Reiss (Crowell, 1972); *Anne Frank: The Diary of a Young Girl* (Doubleday, 1967); and *The Children We Remember*, about Nazi death camp victims, by Chana Byers Abells (Greenwillow, 1986).

Nature books are often among the first we share with our children. Here are some beautifully written and illustrated titles: Alice and Martin Provensen's *The Year at Maple Hill Farm* (Aladdin, 1978), *A Peaceable Kingdom: The Shaker Abecedarius* (Puffin, 1978), and *A Book of Seasons* (Random House, 1978); *Miss Rumphius*, written and illustrated by Barbara Cooney (Viking, 1982); *Children of the Forest* by Elsa Beskow (Floris Books, Edinburgh, 1982); *The Midnight Farm*, by Reeve Lindberg, illustrated by Susan Jeffers (Dial Books for Young Readers, 1987); *The Snowy Day*, by Ezra Jack Keats (Viking, 1962); Robert McCloskey's *Blueberries for Sal* (Viking, 1948) and *One Morning in Maine* (Viking, 1952); *The Very Hungry Caterpillar*, by Eric Carle (Philomel, 1969); *The Weaver's Gift*, the story of wool from sheep to blanket (Warner, 1981), and *Sugaring Time* (Aladdin, 1983), about a Vermont family making maple syrup, both by Kathryn Lasky, illustrated with photographs by Christopher G. Knight; *The Lorax*, by Dr. Seuss (Random House, 1971); *The Gift of the Willows*, by Helena Clare Pittman (Minneapolis: Carolrhoda Books, 1988).

Older children enjoy *All Things Bright and Beautiful*, by James Herriot (St. Martin's, 1974); *Old Yeller*, by Fred Gipson (Harper and Row, 1964); *The Wind in the Willows*, by Kenneth Grahame, illustrated E. H. Shepard (Scribners, 1908); *The Call of the Wild*, by Jack London (Grosset and Dunlap, 1965); *The Story of Brother Francis*, by Lene Mayer-Skumanz (Ave Maria Press, 1983); and *The Education of Little Tree*, by Forrest Carter (University of New Mexico Press, 1976). Finally, two less lyrical but very practical guides to new ways of relating with nature are *50 Simple Things Kids Can Do to Save the Earth*, by The EarthWorks Group (Andrews and McMeel, 1990), and *The Sierra Club Summer Book* by Linda Allison (Sierra Club/Scribners, 1977).

Books about **holidays** and **celebrations** can be resources in planning and also provide reading material for home rituals. Try *The Nativity*, retold by Juliana Bragg, illustrated by Sheilah Beckett (Golden, 1982); *Amahl and the Night Visitors*, by Gian Carlo Menotti, illustrated by Michele Lemieux (Morrow, 1986); *Spirit Child: A Story of the Nativity*, by John Bierhorst, illustrated by Barbara Cooney (Morrow, 1984); *A Child Is Born: The Christmas Story*, by Elizabeth Winthrop, illustrated by Charles Mikolaycak (Holiday, 1983); *A Child's Christmas in Wales*, by Dylan Thomas, illustrated by Trina Schart Hyman (Holiday, 1985); *The Best Christmas Pageant Ever*, by Barbara Robinson, illustrated by Judith Gwyn Brown (Harper and Row, 1972); *What a Morning! The Christmas Story in Black Spirituals*, selected and edited by John Langstaff, illustrated by Ashley Bryan (Macmillan, 1987); *The*

Appendix . . .

Gift of the Magi, by O. Henry, illustrated by Lisbeth Zwerger (Picture Book Studio, 1982); *The Clown of God*, by Tomie de Paola (Harcourt Brace Jovanovich, 1978); *A Christmas Carol* by Charles Dickens, illustrated by Trina Schart Hyman (Holiday, 1983); *The Power of Light: Eight Stories for Hanukkah* by Isaac Bashevis Singer, illustrated by Irene Lieblich (Farrar, Straus and Giroux, 1980) and *Celebration: The Book of Jewish Festivals* (Jonathan David, 1987); *Ask Another Question: The Story and Meaning of Passover*, by Miriam Chaikin, illustrated Marvin Friedman (Clarion, 1985); also *Light Another Candle* for Hanukkah, *Make Noise, Make Merry* for Purim, and *Shake a Palm Branch* for Sukkot; *Holiday Tales of Sholom Aleichem* by Sholom Aleichem, illustrated Thomas diGrazia (Aladdin, 1979); *Turkeys, Pilgrims and Indian Corn: The Story of the Thanksgiving Symbols*, by Edna Barth, illustrated by Ursula Arndt (Clarion, 1975); *Celebrations, A Circle of Seasons*, by Myra Cohn Livingston, illustrated by Leonard Everett Fisher (Holiday, 1985); *The Book of Holidays Around the World*, by Alice van Straalen (E. P. Dutton, 1986); and *A Time to Keep: The Tasha Tudor Book of Holidays* (Checkerboard Press, 1977).

BIBLE STORIES

One six-year-old girl who was learning to read imagined all the books she would eventually conquer. "I'm going to read *Charlotte's Web*," she said dreamily, "and *Little House on the Prairie*. But I'll never read the Bible. It's the hardest book in the entire world!" If our child seems to see the Bible as an intimidating tome, we can read the stories one at a time from individual books. Many are included in the following list, which includes recommended editions of stories in the Hebrew scriptures and the New Testament, as well as illustrated children's Bibles.

Madeleine L'Engle's elegant prose and poetry rendition of

the Hebrew scriptures, *Ladder of Angels*, with vividly colored illustrations by children from around the world, is appealing for children and adults; *The Book of Adam to Moses*, by Lore Segal and Leonard Baskin (Schocken, 1987) is also a book to treasure. Isaac B. Singer's *Why Noah Chose the Dove* (Farrar, Straus and Giroux, 1974), Marilyn Hirsh's *Tower of Babel* (Holiday, 1981), and Lillian Freehof's *Stories of King David* (Jewish Publication Society, 1952) are also recommended. *Two-Minute Bible Stories*, retold by Pamela Broughton (Golden, 1990), is an eminently practical read-aloud edition of the Hebrew scriptures.

One of the most readable, human editions of the Christian Bible is *The Crossroad Children's Bible*, translated from the Dutch, with attractive illustrations, colloquial language, and touches of humor (1989). Another popular version is *The Picture Bible* (Chariot Books—David C. Cook), a comic-book version available in hardcover and paper, and in a mini-version containing excerpted stories called *Great Adventures from the Bible* (Chariot Books, 1984). Other attractive editions are *Catherine Marshall's Story Bible*, illustrated by children from around the world (Crossroad, 1982); *The Doubleday Illustrated Children's Bible*, by Sandol Stoddard, paintings by Tony Chen (1983); *The Beginner's Bible* as told by Karyn Henley, illustrated by Dennas Davis (Sisters, Oregon: Questar Publishers, Inc.), an illustrated volume for beginning readers (1989). For older children, *The Adventure Bible: The NIV Study Bible for Kids* (Zondervan, 1989) includes brief explanations of customs and cultural differences. If you are looking for short bedtime stories, *The Macmillan Book of 366 Bible Stories*, retold by Roberto Brunelli, illustrated by Chris Rothero (1988), is packed with lively, satisfying vignettes.

For individual Bible stories, try the Silver Burdett series, including *David and Goliath*, *Noah and the Ark*, *Daniel in the Lions' Den*, *Jonah and the Great Fish*, and more; these are suitable for reading aloud or for skilled readers. Also see the Ladybird Bible Stories, such as *Noah's Ark*, imported from the United Kingdom. And Peter Spier's mostly wordless *Noah's Ark* (Doubleday, 1977) offers parent and child the opportunity to tell the story together.

If you are uncomfortable with Bible stories or are just beginning to explore spirituality with your child, you may prefer a book such as *What Is God?* by Etan Boritzer, illustrated by Robbie Marantz (Firefly, 1990).

MUSIC

"A person who gives this some thought and yet does not regard music as a marvellous gift of God," Martin Luther is supposed to have said, "must be a clodhopper indeed, and does not deserve to be called a human being, but should be permitted to hear nothing but the braying of asses and the grunting of hogs."

Fortunately, most adults and children do respond to the sacred quality of music, even when its theme is not explicitly religious. I can recall one Friday afternoon when two four-year-old boys and a two-year-old girl were running wild around our living room. Before they bumped heads, I walked over to the stereo and put on the William Tell overture. The racetrack music suited their frantic pace, and the three children galloped around the sofa at breakneck speed. Then, when the tempo slowed, they began to walk. Soon all three were sitting on the floor in rapt silence as the rich orchestral sound swelled around them. The music had brought them back to center.

Not only does music touch our hearts, but it can also help us connect with others in the wider world community. Through folk songs and ethnic music, we are drawn closer to all God's children in a language we can understand. Recorded environmental sounds bring distant creatures into our living room so that they become familiar to us. And if we and our kids sing along—or imitate whale sounds and coyote calls—our connections can only grow deeper. As Saint Augustine wrote, to sing is to pray twice.

The following recordings are available on audio tape and, in some cases, compact disc. For catalogues, see Resources for Further Exploration.

For a soothing start to a period of "quiet time" or guided imagery, try Daniel Kobialka's *When You Wish Upon a Star: Relaxation Music for Children* (Li-sem Enterprises, Belmont, California); *Synchestra: Mother Earth's Lullabye* (Elfin Music Company, Camden, Maine); *Festival of Light* by The New Troubadours (Music for Little People); *Good Morning, Good Night* by Kathy & Milenko, Nancy Rumbel & Friends; and Libana's *A Circle Is Cast*.

When you'd like to share some enjoyable, lively music with loving lyrics, here's a selection of recordings: *Teaching Peace* by Red Grammer (Smilin' Atcha Music, Peekskill, New York); *Peter, Paul and Mommy*; Fred Rogers's song albums (*Won't You Be My Neighbor*, *Let's Be Together Today*, *You Are Special*, and *A Place of Our Own*); anything by Raffi (*Singable Songs*, *More Singable Songs*, *Baby Beluga*, *Corner Grocery Store*, *Rise and Shine*, *One Light*, *One Sun*, and *Everything Grows*); *Kiddin' Around* (Favorite Songs from Music for Little People); Sweet Honey in the Rock: *All for Freedom*; *Peace Is the World Smiling: A Collaboration of Concerned Artists* (with songs by Pete Seeger, Taj Mahal, Tickle Tune Typhoon and others, including children); Tom Chapin's *Family Tree*; *Earthmother Lullabies* (volumes 1, 2, and 3); The Barolk Folk's *Joy After Sorrow*, *Angel's Draught*, and *Princess Royal*; *Shake It to the One You Love: Play Songs & Lullabies from Black Musical Traditions*. The Paul Winter Consort's *EarthBeat*, *Concert for the Earth*, *Whales Alive*, *Missa Gaia/Earth Mass*, *Canyon*, and others feature a unique blend of new music, ethnic rhythms, and recorded environmental sounds.

For international music, Nonesuch offers a wide range of

recordings from around the world. On the Music for Little People EarthBeat! label, see *Africa, Jazayer* (Middle Eastern), *Nisava* (Eastern European), *Mañana Para Los Niños* by la Orquesta Batachanga (Afro-Cuban), and two Indian albums, *Flying Beyond* and *Live in India.*

Sharing classical selections, if you enjoy them, is a way of opening a child's heart to a world beyond that which words can express. Vivaldi's *Four Seasons*; Tchaikovsky's *1812 Overture*, *Sleeping Beauty*, and *Nutcracker Suite*; Rossini's *William Tell Overture*; Dukas's *Sorcerer's Apprentice*; Handel's *Water Music*; Saint-Saens's *Carnival of the Animals*; Grieg's *Peer Gynt*; and Dvořak's *"New World" Symphony* are often popular with children; choose your favorite recording. If your child is a baby, hold him while you listen quietly, or "dance" together cheek-to-cheek. If he is older you need not worry about teaching your child the names of the pieces or the composers; just let him listen to the stereo while he plays with blocks or makes a crayon drawing.

BIBLE VIDEOTAPES

"My fundamentalist sister-in-law used to send my son Bible videos on a regular basis," said one mother of a five-year-old. "He loved them because they were so action-packed, but I'm not sure that their approach is what I want to offer him." She had pinpointed the greatest drawback to audio- and videotaped stories: unlike a read-aloud book, the tale is not mediated by a parent's viewpoint. Nor is it presented in the context of a loving, shared experience. For this reason it is important to remain within earshot and be sensitive to your child's responses. And before you buy or rent a particular Bible story on videotape, you may wish to *read* the story and reflect on whether it seems appropriate for your child at this time.

. . . Appendix

As of this writing there are two widely available series of Bible videotapes on the market. The "Superbook" series has lively action, complete with a time machine and two contemporary children who accompany the viewer and offer helpful explanations (from a Christian point of view) throughout. Although some parents may be uncomfortable when the characters stop to "editorialize" with comments on God's will, and the stories are complex enough to occasionally confuse younger viewers, children enjoy these videos.

More recently Hanna-Barbera, better known for *The Flintstones* and other popular cartoons, has produced a series of Bible videotapes called "Great Adventures." Each tape begins with two archaeologists and their comical friend who fall into a cave that eventually leads to ancient times. Although these contemporary "commentators" can seem occasionally intrusive to adults, their remarks keep the children's interest and help explain the action. Technically, these videotapes are of very high quality; the characters are down-to-earth, and not infrequently—in the Genesis and Nativity stories, for example—the animation is lyrical and moving. (Abingdon Press of Nashville, Tennessee, publishes a series of companion books with illustrations from the Hanna-Barbera videotapes.)

Audiotaped Bible stories are also widely available. Look for the Bible Play-Along series produced by Rainfall, Inc. (Grand Rapids, Michigan), which features packaged sets containing an audiotaped story and a related toy (*Esther The Courageous Queen*, for example, comes with an Esther doll, and there is a Jonah with a big fish, etc.). Also recommended are the Bible Time Stories Series, produced by Hosanna Enterprises (David C. Cook), straightforward narrations with musical accompaniment. Many of the latter are narrated by Burl Ives.

RESOURCES FOR
FURTHER EXPLORATION

ON THE SPIRITUAL NURTURE OF CHILDREN:

Berends, Polly Berrien. *Whole Child/Whole Parent*. San Francisco: Harper and Row, 1987.

Cavalletti, Sofia. *The Religious Potential of the Child*. Ramsey, New Jersey: Paulist Press, 1983.

Coles, Robert. *The Spiritual Life of Children*. Boston: Houghton Mifflin, 1990.

Fowler, James. *The Stages of Faith*. San Francisco: Harper and Row, 1981.

Goldman, Ronald. *Readiness for Religion*. New York: The Seabury Press, 1968.

Groome, Thomas H. *Christian Religious Education*. San Francisco: Harper and Row, 1980.

Kushner, Harold S. *When Children Ask About God*. New York: Schocken Books, 1989.

McCarroll, Tolbert. *Guiding God's Children*. New York/Ramsey: Paulist Press, 1983.

Taylor, JoAnne. *Innocent Wisdom*. New York: Pilgrim Press, 1989.

Westerhoff, John. *Will Our Children Have Faith?* New York: The Seabury Press, 1976.

Appendix . . .

ON THE SPIRITUAL LIFE:

Buber, Martin. *I and Thou*. New York: Charles Scribner's Sons, 1970.

Fowler, Jim, and Sam Keen. *Life Maps*. Minneapolis: Winston Press, 1978.

Fox, Matthew. *On Becoming a Musical Mystical Bear*. Paulist Press, 1976.

————. *Original Blessing*. Santa Fe: Bear & Company, 1983.

Herrigel, Eugen. *Zen in the Art of Archery*. New York: Vintage, 1971.

Heschel, Abraham Joshua. *The Insecurity of Freedom*. New York: Farrar, Straus and Giroux, 1966.

Kushner, Harold. *Who Needs God?* New York: Summit, 1989.

L'Engle, Madeleine. *A Circle of Quiet*. San Francisco: Harper and Row, 1977.

————. *The Irrational Season*. San Francisco: Harper and Row, 1977.

May, Gerald. *Care of Mind, Care of Spirit*. San Francisco: Harper and Row, 1982.

Otto, Rudolph. *The Idea of the Holy*. New York: Oxford University Press, 1970.

Peck, M. Scott. *The Road Less Traveled*. New York: Simon & Schuster, 1978.

ON FAMILY AND COMMUNITY:

Bellah, Robert, et al. *Habits of the Heart*. University of California Press, 1985.

Boulding, Elise. *One Small Plot of Heaven*. Wallingford, Pa.: Pendle Hill Publications, 1989.

Boyer, Ernest, Jr. *Finding God at Home*. San Francisco: Harper and Row, 1984.

Bradshaw, John. *Homecoming: Reclaiming and Championing Your Inner Child*. New York: Bantam Books, 1990.

. . . Appendix

Buber, Martin. *I and Thou*. New York: Charles Scribner's Sons, 1970.

Carter, Forrest. *The Education of Little Tree*. Albuquerque: University of New Mexico Press, 1989.

Carey, Diana, and Judy Large. *Festivals, Family and Food*. Gloucestershire: Hawthorn Press, 1982.

Cowan, Paul, with Rachel Cowan. *Mixed Blessings: Overcoming the Stumbling Blocks in an Interfaith Marriage*. New York: Penguin Books, 1987.

Haley, Alex. *Roots*. Garden City: Doubleday, 1974.

Hauerwas, Stanley. *A Community of Character*. South Bend, Ind.: University of Notre Dame Press, 1981.

Lindbergh, Anne Morrow. *Gift of the Sea*. New York: Random House, 1978.

McGinnis, Kathleen and James. *Parenting for Peace and Justice: Ten Years Later*. Maryknoll, N.Y.: Orbis, 1990.

———— and Barbara Oehlberg. *Starting Out Right*. Oak Park, Ill.: Meyer-Stone Books, 1988.

Potok, Chaim. *The Chosen*. New York: Simon & Schuster, 1967.

ON STORIES AND STORYTELLING:

Allison, Christine. *I'll Tell You a Story, I'll Sing You a Song*. New York: Delacorte Press, 1987.

Bausch, William J. *Storytelling: Imagination and Faith*. Mystic, Conn.: Twenty-third Publications, 1988.

Bettelheim, Bruno. *The Uses of Enchantment*. New York: Knopf, 1976.

Campbell, Joseph. *The Hero with a Thousand Faces*. Princeton: Princeton University Press, 1973.

Coles, Robert. *The Call of Stories*. Boston: Houghton Mifflin, 1989.

Appendix . . .

THINGS TO DO WITH CHILDREN:

Cornell, Joseph. *Sharing Nature with Children*. Nevada City, Calif.: Dawn Publications, 1979.

————. *Sharing the Joy of Nature*. Nevada City, Calif.: Dawn Publications, 1989.

Katz, Adrienne. *Naturewatch*. Addison-Wesley, 1986.

Lappé, Frances Moore. *What to Do After You Turn Off the TV*. New York: Ballantine, 1985.

Singer, Dorothy G. and Jerome L. *Make Believe*. Scott, Foresman and Company, 1985.

Sisson, Edith A. *Nature with Children of All Ages*. Englewood Cliffs, N.J.: Prentice Hall Press, 1982.

Tucker, Kristin M., and Rebecca Lowe Warren. *Celebrate the Wonder: A Family Christmas Treasury*. New York: Ballantine/Epiphany, 1988.

Wiseman, Ann. *Making Things: The Hand Book of Creative Discovery*. Boston and Toronto: Little, Brown and Company, 1973.

ON PRAYER:

Boulding, Elise. *Children and Solitude*. Pendle Hill Pamphlet 125, Wallingford, Pennsylvania, 1983.

Hendricks, Gay, and Russel Wills. *The Centering Book*. New York: Simon and Schuster, 1975.

Murdock, Maureen. *Spinning Inward*. Boston & London: Shambhala, 1987.

Nouwen, Henri. *With Open Hands*. Notre Dame, Ind.: Ave Maria Press, 1972.

The Oxford Book of Prayer, ed. J. Appleton. New York: Oxford University Press, 1985.

Today's Gift: Daily Meditations for Families. New York: Hazelden Meditation Series, Harper and Row, 1985.

...Appendix

RELATED SUBJECTS:

Berry, Thomas. *The Dream of the Earth*. San Francisco: Sierra Club Books, 1988.

Coles, Robert. *The Moral Life of Children*. Boston: Atlantic Monthly Press, 1986.

Erikson, Erik. *Childhood and Society*. New York: W.W. Norton & Company, 1963.

Fraiberg, Selma H. *The Magic Years*. New York: Charles Scribner's Sons, 1959.

Frankl, Viktor E. *Man's Search for Meaning*. New York: Washington Square Press, 1984.

Fromm, Erich. *The Art of Loving*. New York: Bantam Books, 1970.

Jung, C. G. *Modern Man in Search of a Soul*. New York: Harcourt Brace & World, 1933.

Macy, Joanna Rogers. *Despair and Personal Power in the Nuclear Age*. Philadelphia: New Society, 1983.

Maslow, Abraham H. *Religions, Values, and Peak-Experiences*. Columbus: Ohio State University Press, 1964.

Miller, Alice. *The Drama of the Gifted Child*. New York: Basic Books, 1981.

Montessori, Maria. *The Montessori Method*. New York: Schocken, 1964.

Nollman, Jim. *Spiritual Ecology*. New York: Bantam Books, 1990.

Pearce, Joseph Chilton. *The Magical Child*. New York: E. P. Dutton, 1977.

Piaget, Jean. *The Construction of Reality in the Child*. New York: Ballantine Books, 1954.

The Quaker Reader, ed. Jessamyn West. New York: Viking, 1962.

Wiesel, Elie. *Night*. New York: Bantam Books, 1986.

Appendix...

MAIL-ORDER SOURCES:

Alcazar Records
Box 429 Dept. 827
South Main Street
Waterbury, VT 05676
(802) 244-8657

Chinaberry Book Service
(books and recordings)
2780 Via Orange Way
Suite B
Spring Valley, CA 92078

Hearth Song catalog
(toys, books, and music)
P.O. Box B
Sebastopol, CA 95473-0601
(800) 325-2502

Music for Little People
(recordings)
Box 1460
Redway, CA 95560
(800) 346-4445

The Nature Company
(books and nature toys)
P.O. Box 2310
Berkeley, CA 94702
(800) 227-1114

Save the Children's Craft Shop
3200 South 76th Street
P.O. Box 33902
Philadelphia, PA 19142-0900
(800) 456-2723

COMMUNITY CONTACTS:

Bread for the World
(lobbying organization on hunger
issues; provides factual educational materials on hunger from
a Christian perspective)
802 Rhode Island Avenue, N.E.
Washington, DC 20018
(202) 269-0200

Children's Creative Response to
Conflict
(resources and workshops for
parents and teachers)
Fellowship of Reconciliation
Box 271
Nyack, NY 10960
(914) 358-4601

The Children's Defense Fund
(an advocacy group for children
who are poor or physically
challenged)
122 C Street, N.W., Fourth Floor
Washington, DC 20001
(202) 628-8787

National Parenting for Peace
and Justice Network
4144 Lindell Blvd.
St. Louis, MO 63108
(314) 533-4445

... Appendix

Oxfam America
Educational Resources
115 Broadway
Boston, MA 02116
(800) 225-5800

United Nations Environmental
Programme
(Environmental Sabbath
materials)
Two U.N. Plaza
New York, NY 10017

Save the Children
54 Wilton Road
Westport, CT 06880
(800) 243-5075

U.S. Committee for UNICEF
475 Oberlin Avenue South
CN 2110
Lakewood, NJ 08701
(800) FOR-KIDS

What a joy it has been to hear from so many readers who have written to share their thoughts, experiences, and challenges. If you'd like to write to me, find out about workshops for your church, synagogue, or school, or receive a copy of my newsletter, please write:

Generation to Generation:
A Network for Families' Spiritual Nurture
P.O. Box 146
Millwood, NY 10546